EARTH
KNOWLEDGE
GENIUS!

Penguin Random House

DK Delhi

Senior Editor Suefa Lee
Senior Art Editor Vikas Chauhan
Editorial Team Nandini D. Tripathy, Ankita Gupta, Janashree Singha
Design Team Baibhav Parida, Sifat Fatima, Revati Anand, Bhavnoor Kaur
Jacket Designer Vidushi Chaudhry
Senior Jacket Designer Suhita Dharamjit
Senior Jackets Editorial Coordinator Priyanka Sharma
Senior DTP Designer Vishal Bhatia
DTP Designers Nand Kishor Acharya, Rakesh Kumar
Project Picture Researchers Geetika Bhandari, Shubham Rohatgi
Pre-Production Manager Balwant Singh
Production Manager Pankaj Sharma
Picture Research Manager Taiyaba Khatoon
Managing Editor Soma B. Chowdhury
Managing Art Editor Govind Mittal
Editorial Head Glenda Fernandes
Design Head Malavika Talukder

DK London

Senior Editor Ashwin Khurana
Project Art Editor Kit Lane
Senior US Editor Kayla Dugger
Senior Cartographic Editor Simon Mumford
Editorial Assistant Binta Jallow
Jacket Design Development Manager Sophia MTT
Production Editors Robert Dunn, George Nimmo
Senior Production Controller Samantha Cross
Managing Editor Francesca Baines
Managing Art Editor Philip Letsu
Publisher Andrew Macintyre
Associate Publishing Director Liz Wheeler
Art Director Karen Self
Publishing Director Jonathan Metcalf

First American Edition, 2022
Published in the United States by DK Publishing
1450 Broadway, Suite 801, New York, NY 10018

Copyright © 2022 Dorling Kindersley Limited
DK, a Division of Penguin Random House LLC
22 23 24 25 26 10 9 8 7 6 5 4 3 2 1
001–326777–May/2022

A catalog record for this book
is available from the Library of Congress.
ISBN: 978-0-7440-5071-4

DK books are available at special discounts when purchased in bulk
for sales promotions, premiums, fund-raising, or educational use.
For details, contact: DK Publishing Special Markets, 1450 Broadway,
Suite 801, New York, NY 10018
SpecialSales@dk.com
Printed in UAE

For the curious
www.dk.com

MIX
Paper from
responsible sources
FSC™ C018179

This book was made with Forest Stewardship
Council™ certified paper – one small step
in DK's commitment to a sustainable future.
For more information go to
www.dk.com/our-green-pledge

EARTH
KNOWLEDGE
GENIUS!

Written by: Clive Gifford, Lizzie Munsey, and Ian Fitzgerald
Consultant: David Holmes

DK

CONTENTS

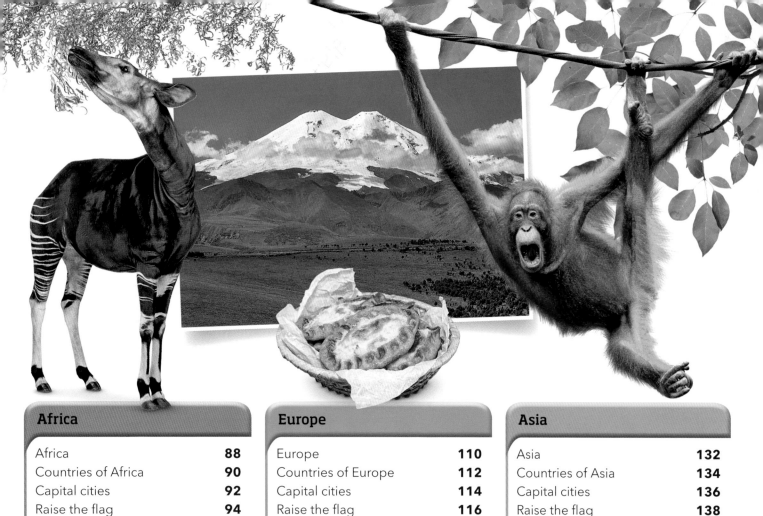

How this book works

Welcome to this fact-packed, quiz-filled challenge. Charge up with some new knowledge and then put your brain to the test by matching the picture clues to the answers. Can you name the deserts around the world? Do you know your capital cities? Can you identify a country from its flag? It is time to find out!

01. Choose your topic. There are seven chapters that introduce you to Earth and take you through each of the six continents. Maybe start with one that you know all about and then move on to something new.

Facts first

First, brush up on the basics with these pages of fun facts. Filled with essential information, they will warm up your brain for the quizzes that follow.

Next, the challenge

Then it's time to test yourself. Take a look at the pictures and the list of answers in the panel at the bottom and try to match them up. Follow these four steps for the best way to tackle things.

54 NORTH AMERICA

① This river connects the Great Lakes with the Atlantic Ocean. It is home to many whale species, including minke and sperm whales.

Montreal's Biosphere Museum lies on the banks of this river.

② Only four bridges cross this 1,980-mile (3,190-km) long river, which runs through Canada and Alaska. It was the main means of transportation during the Klondike Gold Rush in the 19th century.

Measuring 77 miles (124 km), this is the largest lake in Alaska. It is a popular spot for hikers and fishing enthusiasts.

This river flows through the Big Bend National Park.

Bering Sea

HAWAII (USA)

④ More than 100 smaller rivers

This lake holds almost 10 percent of the world's fresh water.

⑦ This iconic river is the longest in North America and runs through 10 states before emptying into the Gulf of Mexico.

...50 ft (594 m), this ...rmed by the ...o 7,700 years ago.

...a de la Maya 12. Rio Celeste 13 Lake Nicaragua
...4. Rio Grande 5. Lake Superior 6. Crater Lake 7. Mississippi River

44 NORTH AMERICA   45

North America

The landmass of North America tapers to the south and Central America, becoming the narrow land bridge to South America. To the east, the Caribbean Sea is speckled with hundreds of warm, tropical islands.

At a glance
Discover some facts and stats about the continent of North America.

In numbers

👪 **Population**
600 million

📐 **Size**
9,233,255 sq miles (24,230,000 sq km)

🧭 **Countries**
23

The Inuit

The Inuit are an Indigenous Arctic population who live in Alaska, Greenland, and the northern Canadian region of Nunavut, which means "our land" in the local language. Inuktitut. This Inuit Nunavut woman is shown in traditional handmade clothing. Hunting is at the core of their culture, and many people in the Nunavut community still practice traditions that date back 5,000 years.

Liberty Island
Rising 305 ft (93 m) from ground level to torch, the iconic statue of the ancient Roman goddess of freedom, Libertas, stands on a small island in New York Bay. A gift from the people of France in 1884, the statue's torch lights the way to freedom.

More than 350 steps take visitors to the observation deck in the statue's crown.

Fantastic festivals
From dazzling fireworks displays to lively street events, North America is filled with amazing celebrations.

Montreal Fireworks Festival
The world's biggest annual fireworks competition is held in La Ronde amusement park in Montreal, Canada, in front of 3 million spectators.

Day of the Dead
Families remember the dead in this Mexican holiday every November. Prayers, traditional foods, music, and dance are all prepared in honor of the deceased.

Junkanoo
In The Bahamas, this spectacular street parade of dance, music, and bright, elaborate costumes celebrates freedom from slavery. It occurs on Boxing Day and New Year's Day.

How to cross the Panama Canal
A shortcut between the Atlantic and Pacific Oceans, the Panama Canal zigzags 51 miles (82 km) through the Central American country of Panama.

01. To use the canal, you need to pay a fee based on the size of your ship. There are also strict schedules, so don't be late!

02. Sets of canal locks (pictured) must be navigated. These locks raise the ship up to 85 ft (26 m) above sea level, allowing you to enter the canal.

03. Once on the canal, your ship travels through Gatun Lake, a large artificial lake that forms a major part of the canal.

04. At the end, a lock will lower you to ocean level. The journey typically takes 8-10 hours. Around 14,000 ships make the trip each year.

I don't believe it
Because Mexico City, Mexico, is using up too much water from under the surface, it is sinking at an approximate rate of 20 in (50 cm) per year.

② **Smallest country by area**
St. Kitts and Nevis are two tiny, paired Caribbean islands that total 100.8 sq miles (261 sq km), smaller than many cities.

① **Biggest country by area**
Canada lies across the northern portion of the continent, occupying 3,855,100 sq miles (9,984,670 sq km).

③ **Biggest city by population**
Mexico City, Mexico, has 9.2 million residents in the city, and more than 21 million in the wider metropolitan area.

⑥ **Biggest lake**
Lake Superior in the US and Canada is 31,700 sq miles (82,097 sq km). It is the most northern lake of the five Great Lakes.

⑤ **Longest river**
The Missouri River flows 2,341 miles (3,766 km) across the US, from the state of Montana to Mississippi.

④ **Highest point**
Denali—formerly known as Mt. McKinley—in the state of Alaska and stands 20,310 ft (6,190 m) high.

⑦ **Lowest point**
The Badwater Basin—large salt flats found in Death Valley in California lie 282 ft (86 m) below sea level.

No peeking
You'll find the answers matched with the numbers of the correct pictures at the bottom of the page.

02. When you have chosen a quiz, take a careful look at the pictures. Can you identify them all? The clues will give you extra information to help you work things out.

03. Look at the "Test Yourself" panel and match the words and pictures. Don't write the answers in the book—you may want to quiz yourself again later to improve your score or give it to a friend to see how they do.

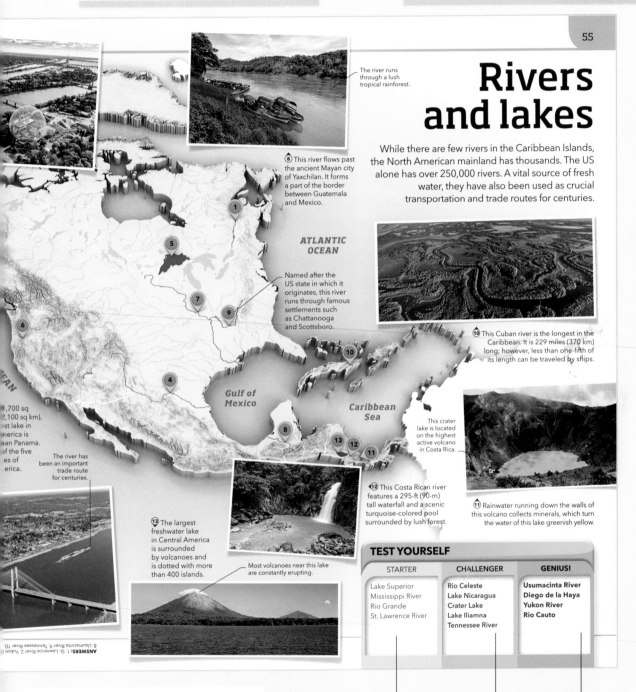

Rivers and lakes

While there are few rivers in the Caribbean Islands, the North American mainland has thousands. The US alone has over 250,000 rivers. A vital source of fresh water, they have also been used as crucial transportation and trade routes for centuries.

The river runs through a lush tropical rainforest.

8 This river flows past the ancient Mayan city of Yaxchilan. It forms a part of the border between Guatemala and Mexico.

ATLANTIC OCEAN

Named after the US state in which it originates, this river runs through famous settlements such as Chattanooga and Scottsboro.

10 This Cuban river is the longest in the Caribbean. It is 229 miles (370 km) long; however, less than one-fifth of its length can be traveled by ships.

Gulf of Mexico

Caribbean Sea

This crater lake is located on the highest active volcano in Costa Rica.

,700 sq 2,100 sq km), st lake in erica is an Panama. of the five es of erica.

The river has been an important trade route for centuries.

12 This Costa Rican river features a 295-ft (90-m) tall waterfall and a scenic turquoise-colored pool surrounded by lush forest.

11 Rainwater running down the walls of this volcano collects minerals, which turn the water of this lake greenish yellow.

13 The largest freshwater lake in Central America is surrounded by volcanoes and is dotted with more than 400 islands.

Most volcanoes near this lake are constantly erupting.

ANSWERS: 1. St. Lawrence River 2. Yukon 8. Usumacinta River 9. Tennessee River 10.

TEST YOURSELF

STARTER	CHALLENGER	GENIUS!
Lake Superior	Rio Celeste	Usumacinta River
Mississippi River	Lake Nicaragua	Diego de la Haya
Rio Grande	Crater Lake	Yukon River
St. Lawrence River	Lake Iliamna	Rio Cauto
	Tennessee River	

04. Work your way through the three levels of difficulty—it's not supposed to be easy! When you think you have gotten them all, check the answers—they are upside down at the bottom of the page.

Start off easy ... These answers should be the easiest to work out.

Getting harder ... How about these harder answers? Can you match them, too?

Truly tricky If you can figure out these final answers, it's official— you're a genius!

PLANET
EARTH

Our place in the Solar System

Mercury
At 3,031 miles (4,878 km) in diameter, this is the smallest planet, three times smaller than Earth.

Sun

Venus
This is the only planet that spins clockwise. A single day on Venus is almost as long as one year on Earth.

Earth
Known as the "Blue Planet" because of its seas and oceans, Earth is also the densest planet in the Solar System.

Mars
The "Red Planet" Mars is called this because the iron in its soil and atmosphere give it a reddish appearance.

Jupiter
The largest planet in the Solar System, it is 89,000 miles (143,000 km) wide. It is so big that all the other planets could fit inside it!

Saturn
The spectacular rings of this planet are more than 174,000 miles (280,000 km) in diameter and are made of chunks of rocks, ice, and dust.

Third rock from the Sun

The Universe has billions of planets, but Earth is the only one we know of that is capable of supporting life. Our planet is part of a Solar System—the eight planets, their moons, comets, asteroids, rock and dust trapped in the orbit of a star, our Sun.

The outer layer of Earth is called the crust. It is made up of solid rocks and minerals.

What is inside Earth?

Earth was a giant ball of hot rock when it formed 4.5 billion years ago. Today, it is made up of three main layers: a thin, cool outer crust; a thick, hot mantle; and a metallic core (made of nickel and iron) as hot as the surface of the Sun.

Hot iron and nickel form the inner core of Earth.

Swirling currents in the metallic outer core generate Earth's magnetic fields.

Mantle

Orbit and seasons

Our planet is tilted at an angle of 23.5 degrees on its axis. This means that as Earth orbits the Sun, the North and South Poles move closer to and farther away from it, which results in the seasons.

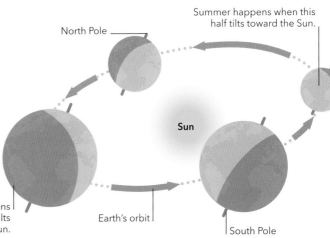

North Pole

Summer happens when this half tilts toward the Sun.

Sun

Winter happens when this half tilts away from the Sun.

Earth's orbit

South Pole

Uranus
Unlike other planets, Uranus rotates on its side. It is the coldest planet in the Solar System, with temperatures of –353°F (–214°C).

Neptune
The most distant planet, Neptune is 2.8 billion miles (4.5 billion km) from the Sun and takes 165 years to orbit it.

I don't believe it!

The rotation of Earth is slowing down, but only gradually. In a billion years, a single day will be 27.5 hours long.

Moon facts

● Scientists think that 4.5 billion years ago, a giant asteroid hit Earth, and the resulting debris from this collision formed the Moon.

● Earth is four times larger than the Moon. The Moon's surface area is smaller than that of Asia.

● The Moon does not produce any light. It only appears bright because it reflects the light from the Sun.

The atmosphere protects Earth by blocking out the Sun's harmful radiation and regulating temperatures.

Earth's atmosphere is made up of layers of gas, such as nitrogen and oxygen.

Earth is the only planet with liquid water. Seas and oceans cover almost 75 percent of its surface.

Types of rocks

Earth's crust is made up of rocks—naturally occurring materials made up of one or more minerals. There are three main types of rocks: igneous, metamorphic, and sedimentary.

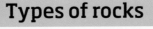

Igneous
When molten volcanic lava cools and solidifies, it forms igneous rocks such as granite.

Metamorphic
These rocks have been changed from one type to another by forces such as intense heat—for example, limestone changing to marble.

Sedimentary
When tiny particles of old rocks build up in layers, the pressure forms sedimentary rocks such as sandstone.

① Its high altitude and northerly position make this the only cold desert in the US. It snows here in winter, though summers are warm and dry.

② North America's largest hot desert is named for a Mexican state, which in turn gives its name to a breed of dog. Although it hardly rains here, it is home to about 3,500 types of plants.

This is the smallest and driest desert in the US. When it gets windy here, the sand vibrates along the dunes and "whistles," giving it the nickname the "singing sands."

④ The world's largest hot desert, it is famous for its dunes and is spread across 11 North African countries.

NASA trains here for its missions to Mars as both have similar harsh environments.

This rocky desert in South America features the mysterious Nazca Lines–vast, ancient drawings in the soil of shapes, animals, and plants.

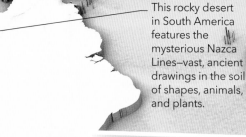

⑥ The driest warm desert on Earth, some parts of it have not seen rain for 400 years! Almost no animals or plants can live here.

⑦ The world's oldest desert, it is 810 miles (1,300 km) long and runs along a coastline. It receives almost no rain, relying on moisture from sea fog.

Deserts

The word "desert" often brings to mind images of sand, but deserts can also be rocky, icy, and even volcanic. Depending on their location, they may be hot or cold, but all receive little or no rainfall. Can you identify these deserts?

⑧ The world's largest desert, made of ice and snow, is spread over 5½ million sq miles (14.2 million sq km). It is the only desert that covers an entire continent.

9) Asia's biggest desert is home to one of the largest sandy areas on Earth. "The empty quarter" in the middle of this desert is larger than France and contains nothing but sand.

10) Blistering summer heat and freezing winters are typical in this rocky desert whose name means "waterless place" in Mongolian.

Bactrian (two-humped) camels are native to this region.

With the biggest oil reserves, this desert is the richest petroleum-producing region in the world.

11) With active volcanoes, hot springs, and yellow sulfur lakes, this desert is located 330 ft (100 m) below sea level.

Also known as the "Sea of Death," this desert is located farther from an ocean than any other.

Desert types
- Hot desert
- Cold desert
- Ice and polar desert

13) Almost 20 million people—many of them sheep herders—live in this region that crosses India and Pakistan, making it the world's most densely populated desert.

14) Although this area is named a desert, it receives too much rainfall to be a true desert. It is covered in unusual red sand, which gets its color from iron oxide.

Acacia trees are one of the more common plants found here.

Grasses help hold the sand together.

15) Named after a British queen, Australia's largest desert has many different landscapes, including sand dunes, salt flats, and rocky plains.

① This North American forest contains a mix of conifers and deciduous trees, which shed their leaves in winter. It has more than 60 tree species, along with animals such as lynx and deer.

② Since 2010, 2.5 million trees, such as oak, birch, and Scots pine, have been planted in this Scottish forest.

White and red pine are among the most common trees here.

Loch Ard is one of 22 small lakes in this forest.

The trees after which this park is named are among the biggest in the world.

③ Located in California's Sierra Nevada mountains, this forest is home to "General Sherman," the world's largest tree by volume, and is between 2,200 and 2,700 years old.

High up in Costa Rica's hills, this forest is usually covered in mist and clouds. Its name means "green mountain" in Spanish.

Ancient monkey puzzle trees are unique to this region.

⑤ Africa's largest forest area covers six countries and includes coastal, lowland, savanna, and swamp woodlands.

African forest buffaloes graze in herds throughout the savanna, as well as lowland rainforests.

The brachystegia trees in this hot, dry forest have evolved to be fire resistant.

Forests

About one-third of Earth's land is covered in forests, but there are many different types depending on climate and the plant life of the region. The three main types of forests are tropical (hot and rainy), temperate (wet in winter and dry in summer), and boreal (cold and dry).

⑥ Located between the Andes Mountains and Peru's Pacific coast, this rainforest is home to alerce trees, which can live for up to 3,500 years.

⑦ Covering seven African countries, this forest is home to about 8,500 types of plants, as well as animals such as giraffes and antelopes.

67 miles going to ohio

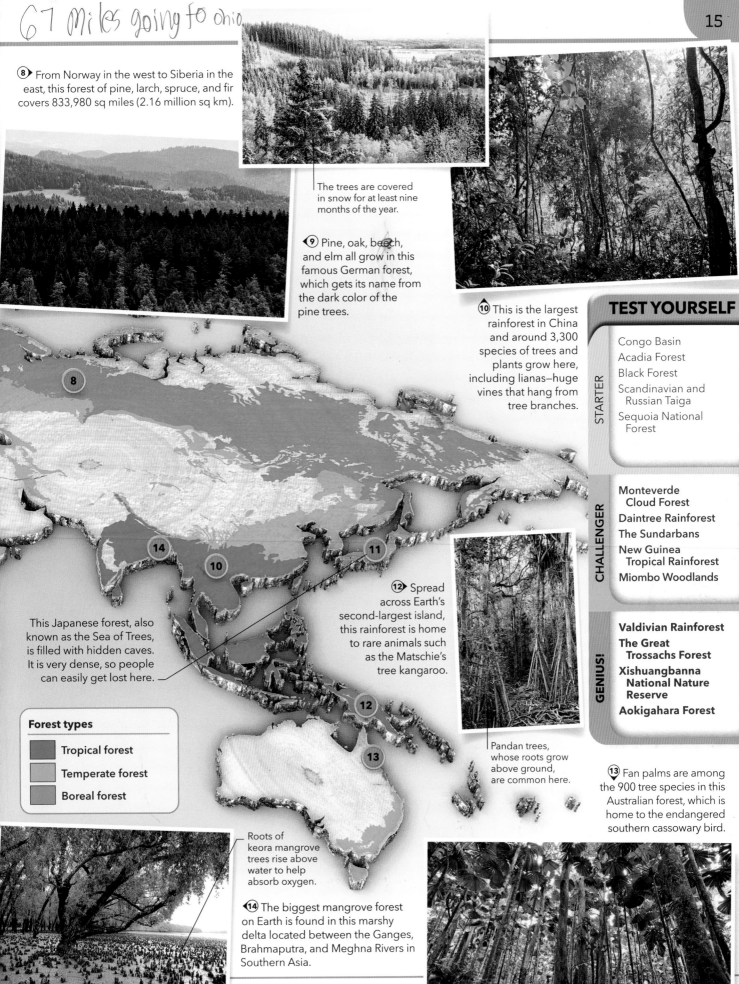

8 From Norway in the west to Siberia in the east, this forest of pine, larch, spruce, and fir covers 833,980 sq miles (2.16 million sq km).

The trees are covered in snow for at least nine months of the year.

9 Pine, oak, beech, and elm all grow in this famous German forest, which gets its name from the dark color of the pine trees.

10 This is the largest rainforest in China and around 3,300 species of trees and plants grow here, including lianas—huge vines that hang from tree branches.

TEST YOURSELF

STARTER
Congo Basin
Acadia Forest
Black Forest
Scandinavian and Russian Taiga
Sequoia National Forest

CHALLENGER
Monteverde Cloud Forest
Daintree Rainforest
The Sundarbans
New Guinea Tropical Rainforest
Miombo Woodlands

GENIUS!
Valdivian Rainforest
The Great Trossachs Forest
Xishuangbanna National Nature Reserve
Aokigahara Forest

This Japanese forest, also known as the Sea of Trees, is filled with hidden caves. It is very dense, so people can easily get lost here.

12 Spread across Earth's second-largest island, this rainforest is home to rare animals such as the Matschie's tree kangaroo.

Pandan trees, whose roots grow above ground, are common here.

Forest types
Tropical forest
Temperate forest
Boreal forest

Roots of keora mangrove trees rise above water to help absorb oxygen.

14 The biggest mangrove forest on Earth is found in this marshy delta located between the Ganges, Brahmaputra, and Meghna Rivers in Southern Asia.

13 Fan palms are among the 900 tree species in this Australian forest, which is home to the endangered southern cassowary bird.

① Stretching 2,983 miles (4,800 km) from Canada down to the US–Mexico border, this range is made up of more than 100 smaller interlinked ranges.

② A natural border between France and Spain, this range contains 9,946 separate mountains. It is also home to the tallest waterfall in France: La Cascade de Gavarnie.

③ Home to the Blue Ridge Mountains, this range also features one of the largest deciduous forests in the world.

Guanacos have a thick, woolly coat that keeps them warm at the high altitude.

This range extends across Austria and Switzerland and six other European countries. Increased pollution makes it the most threatened mountain system in the world.

Villages have grown up in fertile spots of the barren mountain landscape.

⑤ Passing through seven countries, this 4,350-mile (7,000-km) long range is the longest in the world. It contains around 150 active volcanoes.

⑥ This mountain range forms a natural barrier between the Sahara Desert and North Africa's fertile Mediterranean coast.

⑦ Antarctica's highest mountain range is named after the American explorer who discovered it in 1935 while flying over the continent.

⑧ Formed 3.6 billion years ago, these South African highlands are the world's oldest mountains. They are a part of the Barberton Greenstone Belt and contain the oldest volcanic rocks.

Elevation

feet		meters
above 13,123		above 4,000
9,842		3,000
6,560		2,000
3,280		1,000
0		0

Mountain ranges

Most mountains occur in ranges, some of which are hundreds or thousands of miles long. They are formed by either volcanic activity or the movement of the planet's plates over many millions of years. This means that many mountains are still growing—though by only a few millimeters each year.

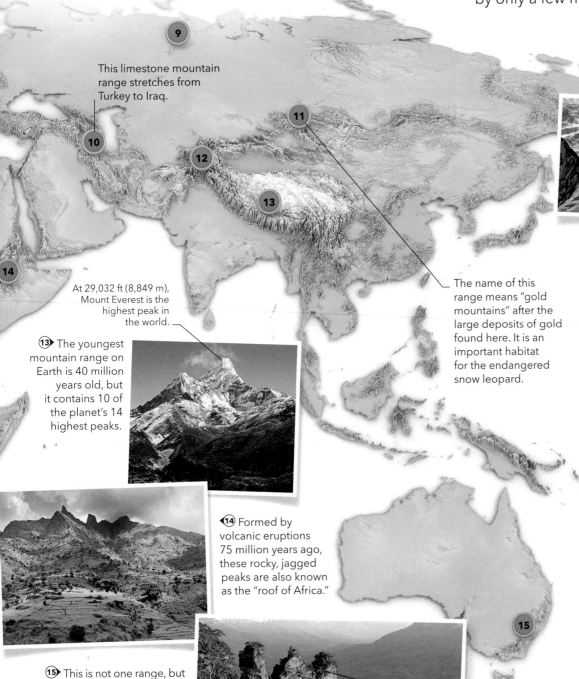

⑨ About 1,553 miles (2,500 km) long, these mountains divide Europe and Asia. In the north of the range, reindeer graze on the tundra.

This limestone mountain range stretches from Turkey to Iraq.

The Fedchenko glacier is the longest nonpolar glacier in the world.

⑫ This mountain range is located mostly in Tajikistan. Its highest peak is 24,590 ft (7,495 m), and during winter, temperatures drop to -58°F (-50°C).

The name of this range means "gold mountains" after the large deposits of gold found here. It is an important habitat for the endangered snow leopard.

At 29,032 ft (8,849 m), Mount Everest is the highest peak in the world.

⑬ The youngest mountain range on Earth is 40 million years old, but it contains 10 of the planet's 14 highest peaks.

⑭ Formed by volcanic eruptions 75 million years ago, these rocky, jagged peaks are also known as the "roof of Africa."

⑮ This is not one range, but a series of linked mountain ranges called a *cordillera* (Spanish for "little rope"). A number of Australia's major rivers originate here.

Peaks such as the Three Sisters are sacred to the nation's Aboriginal Australians.

TEST YOURSELF

STARTER
The Rocky Mountains
The Andes
The Pyrenees
The Alps
The Himalayas

CHALLENGER
Ethiopian Highlands
The Great Dividing Range
Atlas Mountains
The Urals
The Appalachians

GENIUS!
Makhonjwa Mountains
Zagros Mountains
Pamir Mountains
Altai Mountains
Ellsworth Mountains

At the poles

Earth's poles both experience cold, harsh climates. The continent of Antarctica in the south and the Arctic region in the north rarely see temperatures above 32°F (0°C), but both are home to some tough animals, hardy plants, and even a few human-made structures.

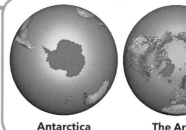

Antarctica   **The Arctic**

① Made entirely of steel and glass, this Brazilian research station contains 17 laboratories and can accommodate up to 64 scientists at a time.

The buildings are flat and long to help withstand high-speed winds.

② Giant skilike feet allow this British research station to be towed across the ice. Their elevated feet are designed to stay above the many feet of expected snowfall.

③ It is dark and freezing cold underneath the ice, but this animal thrives here. It is found in large numbers on the Antarctic seabed.

Clusters grow up to 2 in (5 cm) tall.

④ This is one of only two flowering plants in Antarctica. Because there are no insects here, plants are pollinated by the wind.

Weddell Sea

Antarctic Peninsula

East Antarctica

West Antarctica

Transantarctic Mountains

Ross Sea

This is Earth's southernmost point. In 1911, Norwegian explorer Roald Amundsen became the first human to reach it.

Chicks are born with pale, fluffy feathers that fall out after new, darker ones grow in.

⑥ These flightless birds are expert swimmers. They huddle together in big groups to stay warm.

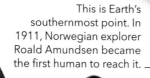

Males grow new antlers every year.

7 Every year, this animal migrates in herds up to 3,100 miles (5,000 km). To survive, it eats lichen from under the snow.

8 This cultural center in Greenland is a meeting place for the Inuit, an Indigenous population that lives across the Arctic.

The flowers face the Sun, following its movement through the sky.

Canada

ARCTIC OCEAN

11

Greenland

ATLANTIC OCEAN

8

14

Russia

9 Thick feathers protect this bird from the cold. It hunts using its sharp claws to snatch up tiny animals hidden under the snow.

10 Tiny hairs on this plant's stem trap heat to prevent it from freezing. Its flowers can be yellow or white.

Earth's northernmost point lies on an ice cap. There is no land under the ice—only the Arctic Ocean.

13 Found across the Arctic, this low-growing shrub with edible fruit is a key source of food for the animal after which it is named.

12 The world's largest meat-eating mammal on land is covered in white fur that is the thickest among all bears and helps it blend into the snow.

14 The northernmost church in Europe is named after the aurora borealis— the natural light display seen in the Arctic.

TEST YOURSELF

STARTER	CHALLENGER	GENIUS!
Polar bear	**Arctic poppy**	**Antarctic pearlwort**
Emperor penguin	**Bearberry**	**Halley VI research station**
Antarctic sea star	**Cathedral of the Northern Lights**	**Comandante Ferraz research station**
Snowy owl	**North Pole**	**Katuaq**
Arctic caribou	**South Pole**	

Energy sources

Earth's sources of energy can be renewable (never run out) or nonrenewable. Renewable sources include the Sun, wind, water, and wood. Coal, oil, and gas, known as fossil fuels because they are made from decomposed organisms that lived millions of years ago, are limited in supply and will eventually run out.

Sun
Light energy from the Sun can be harnessed using solar panels, which can convert it into electricity.

Wind
Wind turbines convert the energy of blowing wind into electricity. This is a cheap and clean form of electricity.

Water
Flowing water from lakes and reservoirs is used to spin turbines and create electricity, known as hydropower.

Wood
Burning wood for fuel is common in some parts of the world, but it adds smoke and pollution to the atmosphere.

Earth's resources

Our planet provides all the resources we need to feed and house ourselves and to provide energy, heat, and light. But we must use Earth's precious resources wisely to sustain them and prevent them from running out and to halt climate change.

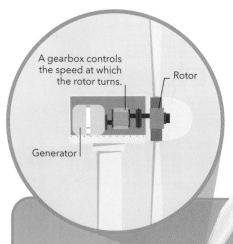

A gearbox controls the speed at which the rotor turns.

Rotor

Generator

How to turn wind into electricity

01. Wind power can be turned into electrical energy using giant windmills, called wind turbines. These are built in areas with strong winds, often on hills or out at sea. When the wind blows, the propellerlike blades of the turbine turn.

02. The blades are connected to a rotor, which is joined to a generator. As the rotor turns, electrical energy is stored in the generator.

04. A substation (small power station) close to the wind farm collects the electricity and sends it via underwater cables to a substation on land. From there, it passes into the local electricity grid, and finally on to homes and businesses.

Coal
Coal is burned at power stations to produce electricity and is a major source of pollution around the world.

Oil
Extracted from deep underground reservoirs by oil rigs, this liquid fossil fuel is used to make gasoline.

Natural gas
Used for heating and cooking, this fuel contains methane and carbon dioxide, which can damage the environment.

Uranium
This radioactive metal is mined from Earth's crust and used to fuel nuclear power stations.

⚒ Flint was the earliest mineral to be mined. It was used to make weapons and tools during the Stone Age.

⚒ Gold was one of the first metals to be mined, found in its purest form on riverbeds alongside sand and gravel.

⚒ Ngwenya Mine, an iron-ore mine on the border of Eswatini in Africa, dates back at least 42,000 years and is believed to be the world's oldest mine.

⚒ The Bingham Canyon copper mine in Utah, the US, is the largest mine in the world. It is 3,182 ft (970 m) deep and more than 2½ miles (4 km) wide.

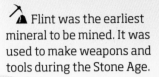

I don't believe it!

It takes a whopping 31 tons (28 metric tons) of prehistoric, 250-million-year-old plant and animal matter to make just ¼ gallon (1 liter) of gasoline.

03. Electrical energy passes down through cables inside the tower.

Deforestation and climate change

The clearing of forests by cutting and burning down trees significantly impacts the environment. Because trees are made up mainly of carbon, destroying them releases carbon dioxide, which is largely responsible for the gradual increase in Earth's temperature. This is known as global warming.

In numbers

191,120 sq miles
(495,000 sq km) The area that would need to be covered in solar panels to supply all of Earth's energy needs. That's almost the size of Spain!

15 million sq miles
(40 million sq km) The forested area across the whole world. We chop down 386,000 sq miles (1 million sq km) every year!

36 billion
The number of barrels of oil produced each year. The US and Saudi Arabia are the world's biggest producers.

Land use

Just over half of Earth's habitable land is used for agriculture. One quarter of this is for growing crops, such as corn, wheat, and rice, and the rest for grazing livestock, such as chickens, sheep, cows, and pigs.

Blue

2 This mineral can be easily identified by its bright color. It is used for making medicine and fertilizers.

yellow

3 Formed when volcanic lava cools, this rock was used to make arrowheads and sharp tools in the past.

black

1 Associated with royalty since ancient times, this precious gemstone is best known in blue, but also comes in purple, yellow, or green. Impurities in this mineral give it its color.

This volcanic rock has a very sharp cutting edge.

Rocks, minerals, and gems

Red

Earth's crust is made up of rocks and minerals. A mineral is made up of just one combination of chemicals, while rocks are a mix of minerals. Gems, or gemstones, are minerals that have been cut and polished and are often rare and valuable. Can you work out which is which from these clues?

4 This blood-red stone is made of the mineral corundum and is widely used in making jewelry.

rocks

This rock can be yellow, white, light gray, or light brown in color.

gold

bruh

The ocean water makes this rock wear away, seen here on Durdle Door, a natural arch in the UK.

This mineral forms in thin layers that look like the rings of a tree.

5 One of Earth's most common rocks, it is used to make stone for building, and if you look closely, you can often see traces of fossils in it.

6 Formed when sheets of volcanic ash build up over millions of years, this stone is used in decorative arts, from marbles to brooches. Its parallel bands can vary in color and thickness.

It is made up of rounded, pea-sized grains called pisoliths.

7 Most of the world's aluminum is made from this spongy-looking rock. It is also used to make cement and steel.

8 People have been making jewelry with this gemstone since the time of the ancient Egyptians, who also crushed it to make eye shadow.

light green

Stripes are formed by the layers in this stone.

Purple

A deep, rich purple is the most valuable shade of this mineral.

9 A type of quartz—a hard, crystal-like mineral—this was used by the ancient Greeks to make wine glasses, as they thought it stopped them from getting drunk.

10 A form of carbon, this gemstone is rare, expensive, and one of the hardest materials found on Earth.

Green White

11 The glittering luster of this mineral means that it is often mistaken for precious gold. It crystallizes to form perfect cubes.

gold crystals

Another mineral, malachite, often forms green stains on this mineral.

Blue green

14 This mineral changes color when it is exposed to rain, wind, or sunlight. Its name comes from the Italian for "sky blue."

12 One of the rarest gems, this precious stone was first found in ancient Egypt. Today, more than half of the world's supply comes from mines in Colombia.

coal

The surface of this rock has a brilliant, metal-like shine.

13 An older and harder form of coal, this rock is almost pure carbon and is used to make a long-lasting and smokeless form of fuel.

rock

15 Making up a quarter of Earth's sedimentary rocks, this rock is made up of tiny, sandlike grains held together by clay and other minerals.

TEST YOURSELF

STARTER
Diamond
Emerald
Limestone
Ruby
Sapphire

CHALLENGER
Azurite
Banded agate
Amethyst
Sandstone
Yellow sulfur

GENIUS!
Anthracite
Bauxite
Malachite
Obsidian
Pyrite

ANSWERS: 1. Sapphire 2. Yellow sulfur 3. Ruby 4. Obsidian 5. Limestone 6. Banded agate 7. Bauxite 8. Malachite 9. Amethyst 10. Diamond 11. Pyrite 12. Emerald 13. Anthracite 14. Azurite 15. Sandstone

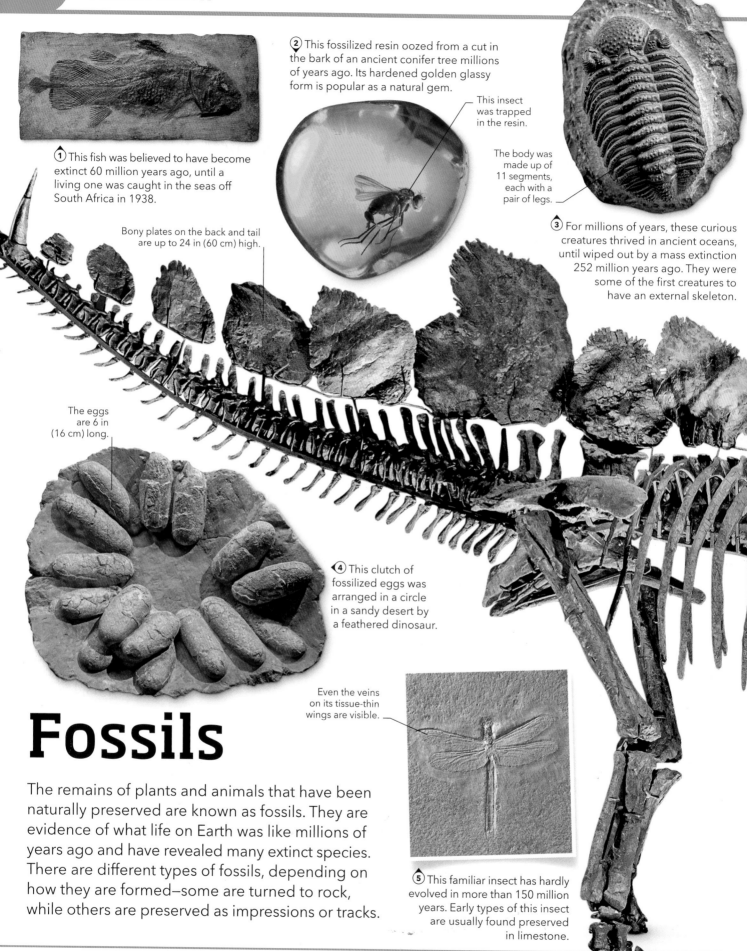

① This fish was believed to have become extinct 60 million years ago, until a living one was caught in the seas off South Africa in 1938.

② This fossilized resin oozed from a cut in the bark of an ancient conifer tree millions of years ago. Its hardened golden glassy form is popular as a natural gem.

This insect was trapped in the resin.

The body was made up of 11 segments, each with a pair of legs.

③ For millions of years, these curious creatures thrived in ancient oceans, until wiped out by a mass extinction 252 million years ago. They were some of the first creatures to have an external skeleton.

Bony plates on the back and tail are up to 24 in (60 cm) high.

The eggs are 6 in (16 cm) long.

④ This clutch of fossilized eggs was arranged in a circle in a sandy desert by a feathered dinosaur.

Even the veins on its tissue-thin wings are visible.

Fossils

The remains of plants and animals that have been naturally preserved are known as fossils. They are evidence of what life on Earth was like millions of years ago and have revealed many extinct species. There are different types of fossils, depending on how they are formed—some are turned to rock, while others are preserved as impressions or tracks.

⑤ This familiar insect has hardly evolved in more than 150 million years. Early types of this insect are usually found preserved in limestone.

ANSWERS: 1. Coelacanth 2. Amber 3. Trilobite 4. Oviraptor eggs 5. Dragonfly 6. Ammonite 7. Theropod footprint 8. Pine cone 9. Pterodactylus 10. Coprolite 11. Petrified tree 12. Stegosaurus

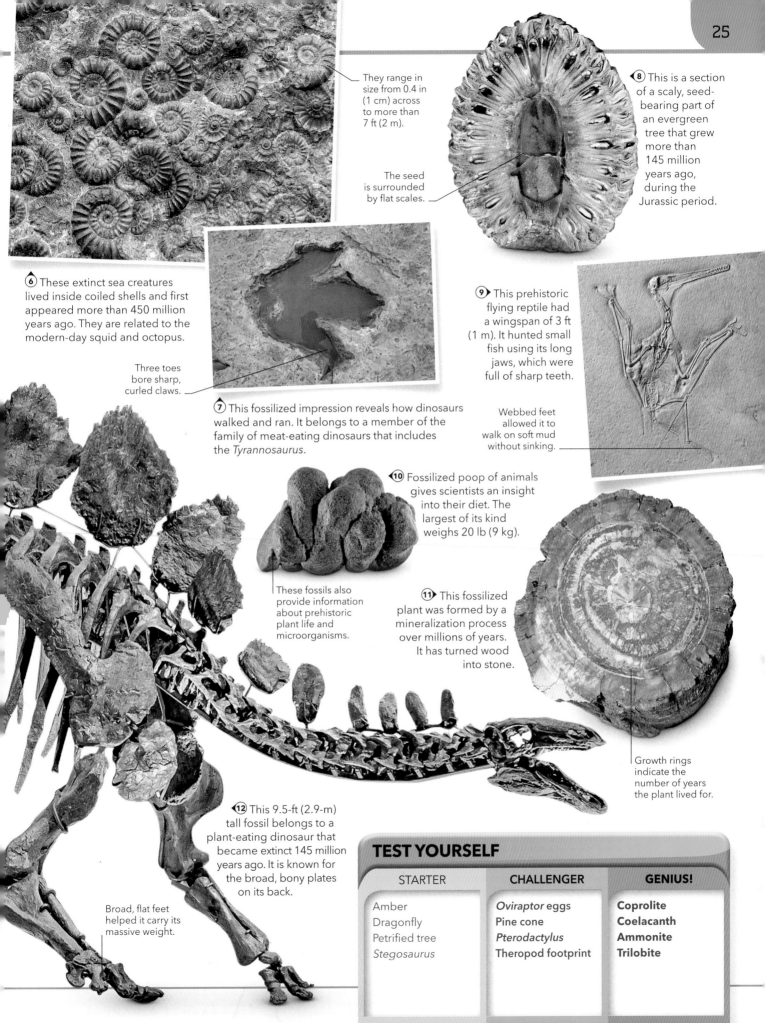

They range in size from 0.4 in (1 cm) across to more than 7 ft (2 m).

The seed is surrounded by flat scales.

8 This is a section of a scaly, seed-bearing part of an evergreen tree that grew more than 145 million years ago, during the Jurassic period.

6 These extinct sea creatures lived inside coiled shells and first appeared more than 450 million years ago. They are related to the modern-day squid and octopus.

Three toes bore sharp, curled claws.

7 This fossilized impression reveals how dinosaurs walked and ran. It belongs to a member of the family of meat-eating dinosaurs that includes the *Tyrannosaurus*.

9 This prehistoric flying reptile had a wingspan of 3 ft (1 m). It hunted small fish using its long jaws, which were full of sharp teeth.

Webbed feet allowed it to walk on soft mud without sinking.

10 Fossilized poop of animals gives scientists an insight into their diet. The largest of its kind weighs 20 lb (9 kg).

These fossils also provide information about prehistoric plant life and microorganisms.

11 This fossilized plant was formed by a mineralization process over millions of years. It has turned wood into stone.

Growth rings indicate the number of years the plant lived for.

12 This 9.5-ft (2.9-m) tall fossil belongs to a plant-eating dinosaur that became extinct 145 million years ago. It is known for the broad, bony plates on its back.

Broad, flat feet helped it carry its massive weight.

TEST YOURSELF

STARTER	CHALLENGER	GENIUS!
Amber	*Oviraptor* eggs	Coprolite
Dragonfly	Pine cone	Coelacanth
Petrified tree	*Pterodactylus*	Ammonite
Stegosaurus	Theropod footprint	Trilobite

Restless planet

Earth's crust is broken up into a number of massive, interlocking pieces called tectonic plates. The movement of magma (molten rock) in the mantle below pushes these plates around. Over millions of years, this movement has caused Earth to change—continents have been created, oceans have opened and closed, and mountains have risen.

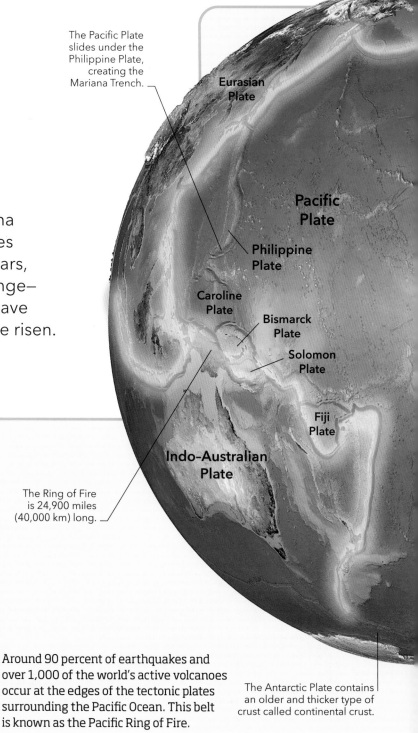

The Pacific Plate slides under the Philippine Plate, creating the Mariana Trench.

Eurasian Plate

Pacific Plate

Philippine Plate

Caroline Plate

Bismarck Plate

Solomon Plate

Fiji Plate

Indo-Australian Plate

The Ring of Fire is 24,900 miles (40,000 km) long.

The Antarctic Plate contains an older and thicker type of crust called continental crust.

Plate boundaries

Where two tectonic plates meet, different types of plate boundaries are formed, based on how the plates move. Plate movement can cause earthquakes and volcanic eruptions.

Transform
At these boundaries, two plates grind past each other. Sudden movements cause earthquakes.

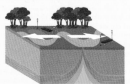

Divergent
At these boundaries, plates move apart, pushed by hot rock welling up from below.

Normal
Also called "dipslip," one plate rises above another at these boundaries.

What is the Ring of Fire?

Around 90 percent of earthquakes and over 1,000 of the world's active volcanoes occur at the edges of the tectonic plates surrounding the Pacific Ocean. This belt is known as the Pacific Ring of Fire.

Measuring earthquakes

An earthquake's power, or magnitude, is measured on the Richter Scale. Each step on the scale is 10 times more powerful than the previous one.

1.0-1.9
These tiny tremors can hardly be felt. They happen almost everywhere all the time.

2.0-2.9
Gentle vibrations are felt. There are around 1 million worldwide each year.

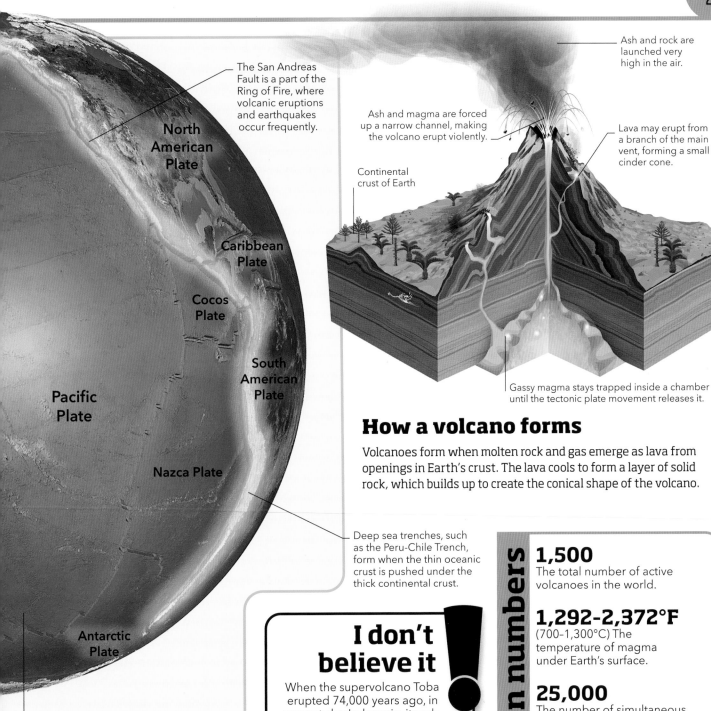

The San Andreas Fault is a part of the Ring of Fire, where volcanic eruptions and earthquakes occur frequently.

North American Plate

Caribbean Plate

Cocos Plate

South American Plate

Pacific Plate

Nazca Plate

Antarctic Plate

The Pacific Plate is the largest plate that is made entirely of oceanic crust. Oceanic crust is thinner but heavier than continental crust.

Ash and rock are launched very high in the air.

Ash and magma are forced up a narrow channel, making the volcano erupt violently.

Lava may erupt from a branch of the main vent, forming a small cinder cone.

Continental crust of Earth

Gassy magma stays trapped inside a chamber until the tectonic plate movement releases it.

How a volcano forms

Volcanoes form when molten rock and gas emerge as lava from openings in Earth's crust. The lava cools to form a layer of solid rock, which builds up to create the conical shape of the volcano.

Deep sea trenches, such as the Peru-Chile Trench, form when the thin oceanic crust is pushed under the thick continental crust.

I don't believe it

When the supervolcano Toba erupted 74,000 years ago, in present-day Indonesia, its ash and dust blocked out the Sun's light across the world for more than six years.

In numbers

1,500
The total number of active volcanoes in the world.

1,292-2,372°F
(700-1,300°C) The temperature of magma under Earth's surface.

25,000
The number of simultaneous nuclear bomb explosions it would take to release energy equal to a magnitude 9.0 earthquake.

3.0-4.9
Earth tremors are more noticeable, but there is little or no damage.

5.0-5.9
These are called "light" earthquakes. Windows may rattle or break.

6.0-7.9
Cracks appear in buildings and roads, and small structures may collapse.

8.0-8.9
Buildings, bridges, and roads collapse. Landslides and tsunamis may occur.

9.0 and above
Major devastation that destroys towns and cities. The worst earthquake ever measured was 9.5.

① America's most destructive volcanic eruption happened in Washington in 1980. The column of ash rose to a height of 12 miles (20 km).

The top 1,300 ft (400 m) of rock was blasted off to form a cloud of debris.

② This Icelandic volcano's eruption in 2010 formed massive ash clouds that grounded planes in Europe for a week. Its name means "island mountain glacier."

The eruption of this Alaskan volcano in 1912 was the biggest of the 20th century.

④ The world's largest active volcano burst through the ocean floor and now towers over Hawaii.

Lava fountains are an everyday sight here.

⑤ A massive eruption of this Guatemalan volcano in 1902 dumped rock and ash over 2,485 miles (4,000 km) away in California.

⑥ Just off the coast of Iceland, this island was formed between 1963 and 1967 by an undersea eruption.

Erupting Earth

Volcanic activity has shaped our planet. Most volcanoes form at the borders of tectonic plates. Some can form very quickly, while others take millions of years. The red triangles on this map mark where the active volcanoes are found today.

⑦ At 22,615 ft (6,893 m), this is the world's highest active volcano, located up in the Andes Mountains, between Chile and Argentina.

8 The Roman cities of Pompeii and Herculaneum were destroyed by the eruption of this volcano in 79 CE.

The Italian city of Naples lies just 5.6 miles (9 km) from this active volcano.

9 Europe's largest active volcano is located on a small island just off the Italian island of Sicily. Its name means "I burn" in ancient Greek.

The volcano is 11,014 ft (3,357 m) tall.

10 One of the biggest eruptions of the 20th century happened in the Philippines in 1991. Luckily, scientists predicted the event and 5,000 people living nearby were evacuated before the blast.

Thick ash rose 21 miles (34 km) in the air and blocked out the Sun for days.

This island volcano off Papua New Guinea erupts on average once every 10 years.

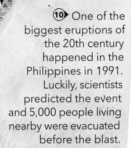

This volcanic eruption in 1883 was one of the loudest explosions in history. The tsunami it caused destroyed nearly 70 percent of the island.

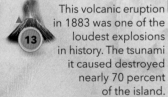

13 With spectacular lava fountains erupting from a 5-mile (8-km) wide crater, this volcano on Réunion Island is one of Earth's most active.

Rivers of molten lava flow down its shallow sides.

14 The eruption of this deadly volcano in Indonesia in 1815 caused a massive loss of human life. Falling volcanic ash destroyed crops, leading to famine.

TEST YOURSELF

STARTER	CHALLENGER	GENIUS!
Krakatoa	Bam	**Mount Pinatubo**
Mauna Loa	Novarupta	**Mount Tambora**
Mount Etna	Santa María	**Ojos del Salado**
Mount St. Helens	Surtsey island	**Piton de la Fournaise**
Mount Vesuvius	Eyjafjallajökull	

② Located on the island of Staffa, Scotland's most famous cave has walls that are made of hexagonal pillars of basalt rock.

③ Elaborate chambers, such as the Chapel of St. Kinga, have been carved out of salt rock inside this old Polish mine.

① Named after the size of its huge caverns, this is the longest known cave system in the world. It extends for more than 400 miles (644 km).

The walls of this cave system are made of limestone.

The columns are around 65 ft (20 m) tall.

TEST YOURSELF

STARTER

Blue Grotto
Hang Son Doong
Marble Caves
Mammoth Cave
Cave of the Crystals

CHALLENGER

Coober Pedy
Fingal's Cave
Waitomo Cave
Batu Caves
Veryovkina Cave
Wieliczka Salt Mine

GENIUS!

Eisriesenwelt Cave
Škocjan Caves
Reed Flute Cave
Carlsbad Caverns
Holqa Sof Omar

④ Discovered in 2000, this cave in Mexico contains the largest crystals ever found—up to 49 ft (15 m) tall and 10 ft (3 m) thick!

Known for their high-roofed chambers and rock formations, these caves in a national park in New Mexico are 4 million years old.

The Cerkevnik Bridge is located 154 ft (47 m) above the river.

The crystals are made of the mineral gypsum.

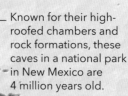

⑥ The Reka River has carved this cave system in Slovenia and flows through some of its deepest chambers.

⑦ Located in Patagonia, Chile, these swirling blue-gray caves have been carved into the base of rocky islands by the crashing waves of Lake General Carrera.

Only the first mile of the cave is covered in ice.

⑧ Extending more than 26 miles (42 km), this Austrian ice cave is the largest in the world. Its name is German for "world of the ice giants."

9 This sea cave off the coast of Capri in Italy is named for the glowing color of its light. It is only accessible by boat.

10 With a main passage big enough to fit a 40-story skyscraper, this cave in Vietnam is the largest in the world.

11 After more than 30 expeditions spread over 50 years, this cave in Abkhazia, Georgia, was declared the deepest cave in the world in 2018.

The cave is partly illuminated by sunlight passing though a huge underwater cavity.

This 180-million-year-old cave in China is named after a type of grass that grows outside it and is used to make a musical instrument.

The caves are dotted with Hindu temples and shrines.

The cave is 7,257 ft (2,212 m) deep.

13 An important site of pilgrimage for Malaysian Hindus, these limestone caves are named after a river that flows nearby.

Located in Ethiopia, this is Africa's longest cave system. It was formed by the Weib River, and is also an important Islamic shrine.

The glow-worms emit light from their tails to attract prey.

15 These ancient limestone caves in New Zealand have a unique natural lighting system—millions of tiny glow-worms!

The walls of this Serbian Orthodox Church have been carved by hand.

16 It was so hot in this Australian mining town that workers moved their houses, shops, and even churches into the underground mine!

Caves and mines

Some of the most impressive sites on Earth can be found underground. These include spectacular hollows and natural rock formations, as well as elaborately designed chambers within human-made mines.

Water works

Life on Earth would not be possible without water. We drink it, use it to wash dishes and clothes, and take a shower with it. In nature, the effects of water can be seen all over the world, from rivers carving out valleys to destructive floods and melting glaciers.

Where is Earth's water ?

Around 71 percent of Earth is covered in water, which is shared by the world in two main forms: salt water and fresh water.

Salty water from oceans and seas makes up 97 percent of Earth's water.

Fresh water from rivers, lakes, ice caps, and underground sources makes up only 3 percent.

What is the water cycle?

Earth always has the same amount of water, but it changes form constantly as it circulates between the sea, sky, and land in a continuous process called the water cycle.

02. As water vapor rises, it cools to form clouds of droplets in a process known as condensation.

Condensation

01. When water is heated by the Sun, it turns into water vapor in a process known as evaporation.

Evaporation

In numbers

69%
The amount of fresh water used for farming. Only 8 percent of the total water consumed in the world each year is used in homes.

One trillion
The amount of water in tons that is evaporated by the Sun every day.

3 billion
The number of people affected by water shortages worldwide.

The power of water

Water has played a very important role in the formation of our planet. Here are some of the ways in which water shapes the landscape.

Wave erosion
Coastlines are worn down, or eroded, continuously by waves crashing against them.

Rain erosion
Heavy rain can wash away earth, stones, and rocks, causing dangerous mudslides and landslides.

Weathering
Substances in rain can dissolve rocks over time, a process known as weathering.

03. Small droplets of water inside clouds join together to form bigger drops that fall as precipitation, such as rain or snow.

Freezing

Precipitation

Melting

04. The water that falls as rain or melts from snow collects in rivers and streams.

05. Some water seeps into the ground and returns to the surface in springs and rivers, which eventually flow back into the ocean.

I don't believe it

When the oceans first formed 3.8 billion years ago, they were not salty. Minerals in the ground and in rain have made them salty over time.

Water facts

- The Atlantic Ocean is saltier than the Pacific Ocean. No one really knows why.
- Water is the only substance on Earth that is found in three forms: liquid (water), solid (snow and ice), and gas (steam and vapor).
- Water is not actually colorless–even the purest water is slightly blue in color.
- You can live a whole month without food but only one week without water.

Saving water

On average, each of us wastes up to 30 gallons (136 liters) of water every day. Taking a few simple steps can really help cut down on this wastage.

Switch to low-flow or low-flush toilets, which use less water than regular full-flush toilets.

Take showers instead of baths, as showers use up about half as much water.

Turn off the faucet while you brush your teeth to save up to 5 gallons (20 liters) each day.

Fill up your washing machine with clothes. A full load uses less water than half a load.

Check your pipes. A single house can lose hundreds of gallons a year in leaks.

Valley formation
As rivers flow, their movement from side to side carves out canyons and river valleys.

Riverbed erosion
The water in a river constantly erodes the riverbed, forming rapids, waterfalls, and lakes.

Deposition
When a river slows down, the mud and silt it is carrying settle to form deltas, basins, and floodplains.

Glaciation
Masses of moving ice, called glaciers, slide slowly downhill from mountains and carve out U-shaped valleys.

Flooding
Excessive rain, overflowing rivers, and tidal waves can flood vast areas of land, sweeping away people and property.

① Located around the North Pole, the smallest and shallowest ocean on Earth is home to narwhals—a type of whale.

Narwhals have a long and spiral single tusklike tooth that helps them hunt underwater.

② This sea separates the UK from the rest of Europe. It is dotted with rigs that drill into its rich oil and gas reserves.

A patch of Neptune seagrass found here is believed to be around 100,000 years old.

③ This sea's name means "the center of the Earth," and it is bordered by 22 countries. This is the only sea where Neptune seagrass— one of the oldest living organisms on Earth— is found.

Surrounded by four huge, circular currents known as ocean gyres, this is the only sea with no land boundaries.

This sea is known for its calm waters.

⑤ The Mississippi River empties into this body of water, which is also home to 49 species of shark. The dangerous bull shark is the most common species found here.

⑥ With an area of around 63 million sq miles (162 million sq km) and a maximum depth of 36,201 ft (11,034 m), this is the largest and deepest ocean in the world.

The world's second largest ocean separates Europe and Africa from the Americas.

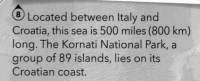

⑧ Located between Italy and Croatia, this sea is 500 miles (800 km) long. The Kornati National Park, a group of 89 islands, lies on its Croatian coast.

⑨ This tropical sea is dotted with more than 7,000 islands, and the colorful Mesoamerican Reef is found here.

Pink gorgonian corals are commonly found in this sea.

Oceans and seas

More than 70 percent of Earth's surface is covered with saltwater in the form of oceans and seas. Some are turbulent and dangerous, while others are calm and full of plants and animals. They all play an essential part in protecting our planet's ecosystem.

10 Sand blowing down from the Gobi Desert turns the surface of this sea yellow, while blooming algae turns it green.

The algae is not toxic and swamps the waters every summer.

11 This sea is an important base for the Russian Navy. The water is low in oxygen, so very little marine life can survive here.

The Palm Jumeirah was built using 3.3 billion ft³ (94 million m³) of sand.

12 Also known as the Arabian Gulf, this water body has large oil reserves under its floor. It is home to the largest artificial island in the world: the Palm Jumeirah in Dubai, UAE.

Named after the vast country that borders it, this sea has some of the world's busiest waterways—one-third of all container ships pass through it each year.

The stone statue of Thiruvalluvar is 133 ft (41 m) tall.

14 This is the world's warmest ocean. A statue of Tamil poet Thiruvalluvar stands on its shore, marking the southernmost tip of the country after which the ocean is named.

15 The Great Barrier Reef lies in this sea that stretches for 1,200 miles (1,930 km) along the eastern coast of Australia.

16 Officially recognized as an ocean in 2021, this freezing-cold body of water is filled with icebergs. It is also known as the Antarctic Ocean.

The Heart Reef is one of this sea's most famous features. Parts of it are 20 million years old.

17 This is one of the world's saltiest seas. At its northern end, the Suez Canal connects it to the Mediterranean Sea, forming a passage between Europe and Asia.

TEST YOURSELF

STARTER
Pacific Ocean
Arctic Ocean
Atlantic Ocean
Indian Ocean
Southern Ocean

CHALLENGER
Red Sea
Yellow Sea
Persian Gulf
Coral Sea
Caribbean Sea
Mediterranean Sea

GENIUS!
Sargasso Sea
Adriatic Sea
Black Sea
South China Sea
North Sea
Gulf of Mexico

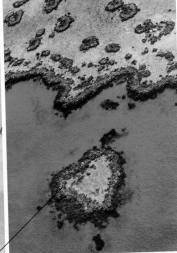

ANSWERS: 1. Arctic Ocean 2. North Sea 3. Mediterranean Sea 4. Sargasso Sea 5. Gulf of Mexico 6. Pacific Ocean 7. Atlantic Ocean 8. Adriatic Sea 9. Caribbean Sea 10. Yellow Sea 11. Black Sea 12. Persian Gulf 13. South China Sea 14. Indian Ocean 15. Coral Sea 16. Southern Ocean 17. Red Sea

Underwater features

In the oceans and seas and underground, some beautiful and curious water features can be found. Some lie in the widest, deepest, and least explored corners of our planet. Can you work out which watery world is which?

At its deepest, this canyon plunges to 207 ft (63 m).

① This underwater crack off Iceland is the only place where you can scuba dive between the European and North American tectonic plates.

ARCTIC OCEAN

ATLANTIC OCEAN

PACIFIC OCEAN

This place resembles a sunken waterfall, caused by currents on the ocean floor. It has a steep drop of 394 ft (120 m).

② Located in Belize, the world's largest underwater sinkhole is 984 ft (300 m) wide and 410 ft (125 m) deep. Inside are water-filled caves full of stalactites.

The circular feature is a hole in the roof of an underwater cave.

Divers can swim between the submerged benches, paths, and a small footbridge.

The largest underwater volcano on Earth formed in 2019 in an explosion so violent that the nearby island of Mayotte shifted 6 in (15 cm) westward.

④ This small 98-ft (30-m) wide brine pool in the Gulf of Mexico is four times saltier than normal seawater. The dissolved methane in its waters poisons everything that swims nearby.

This stretch of sea is popularly called "the underwater garden of Eden."

⑤ In winter, this lake in the Austrian Alps is only 3 ft (1 m) deep. But in summer, melting snow floods it to a depth of 39 ft (12 m). The lake is named for the color of its waters.

The darker sections contain almost no oxygen and get their color from minerals and toxins.

⑥ This seawater inlet between Africa and Asia has more than 1,000 fish species and hundreds of colorful corals.

ANSWERS: 1. Mid-Atlantic Ridge 2. Great Blue Hole 3. Cabo San Lucas Sandfalls 4. The "Jacuzzi of Despair" 5. Grüner See 6. Red Sea 7. Mayotte Volcano 8. Orda Cave 9. Challenger Deep 10. Toyama Bay 11. Zhemchug Canyon 12. Kilsby Sinkhole 13. Jellyfish Lake

9 Earth's deepest point lies in the Mariana Trench, 36,200 ft (11,034 m) under the Pacific Ocean. It is deeper than the height of Mount Everest.

The anglerfish is found in this extreme environment.

8 Located in Russia, this is the largest underwater gypsum cave in the world. The water in it is so clear that divers can see up to a distance of 150 ft (46 m).

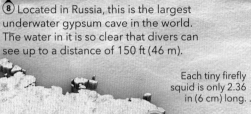

10 Millions of firefly squid can be seen in the middle of the Sea of Japan (East Sea) each year. Their light-emitting tentacles give an amazing view.

Each tiny firefly squid is only 2.36 in (6 cm) long.

PACIFIC OCEAN

The world's largest submarine canyon runs 8,530 ft (2,600 m) under the Bering Sea and fills an area larger than the Grand Canyon.

NDIAN OCEAN

This water-filled limestone cave in the middle of a sheep farm is 197 ft (60 m) deep. It is one of Australia's best scuba diving spots.

SOUTHERN OCEAN

The jellyfish here are harmless because there are no predators to attack them.

13 This water body in Palau, Micronesia, is cut off from the sea but teems with species of jellyfish that were once found only in the ocean.

Weather and climate

Weather is what you experience from day to day—such as Sun or rain. Climate is the average weather in a region over a long period of time and is different across the world. Studying climate patterns helps us understand how the climate is changing.

Types of climates

Different regions have different climates depending on many factors, including their location on Earth, distance from the ocean, and height above sea level. There are five main types of climates, each of which can have many variations.

Tropical
Warm and humid weather with heavy rainfall. This climate encourages the growth of lush rainforests.

Dry
Hot and dry weather with little rainfall. This climate leads to the formation of most deserts.

Warm temperate
Sunny and warm summers and mild winters, with just enough rain for crops and plants to grow.

Cool temperate
Cool summers and mild winters, with plenty of rainfall for the growth of plants and trees.

Arctic
Very cold and very dry weather. This climate leads to the formation of ice sheets.

What is the greenhouse effect?

A layer of gases in the atmosphere traps the Sun's energy and keeps our planet warm enough for life to exist. It acts like the glass roof of a greenhouse, so it is known as the greenhouse effect. However, the level of these gases, known as greenhouse gases, is rising. As a result, more heat is being trapped, causing global warming.

Sun

01. The Sun's heat travels through the atmosphere to Earth's surface.

Earth's atmosphere

Types of clouds

Water evaporates from Earth's surface and then condenses in the atmosphere to form clouds. These clouds affect the weather, help keep Earth warm, and alsoprotect it from too much heat from the Sun. They take on various shapes, all of which bring different types of weather.

Cumulus
These fluffy white clouds are formed when warm air rises into the cool sky. They are often seen on breezy, sunny days.

Cumulonimbus
When cumulus clouds fill up with extra moisture, they grow into these giant clouds seen during thunderstorms.

Stratus
Flat sheets of this type of cloud form closer to the surface on dry days. They can be white or gray, but they do not bring rain.

Stratocumulus
Stratus clouds can come together to form these large, rounded masses that usually bring mild weather.

Weather forecasting

Predicting–or forecasting–the weather is difficult. To do so accurately, experts look for patterns in wind, rainfall, and temperatures. Weather data, including images such as this one, is transmitted by weather satellites orbiting Earth. Data is also gathered from other sources, like land-based weather stations.

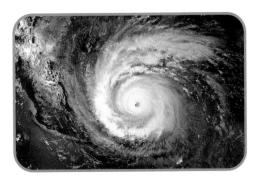

🌎 Melting glaciers are causing sea levels to rise by around 0.1 in (3 mm) every year. By 2100, they could be up to 30 in (76 cm) higher than they are today.

🌎 A global increase in temperatures has led to more frequent extreme weather events, such as flooding.

🌎 An increase of 34.7°F (1.5°C) in the world's average temperature could place almost a quarter of all plant and animal life at risk of extinction.

🌎 Twenty of the hottest years on record have been in the last 22 years.

02. Some of the heat is reflected off the atmosphere.

Some of the heat travels into space.

Greenhouse gases

The heat from the Sun warms Earth.

04. Some heat is trapped by greenhouse gases, increasing global temperatures.

Earth

03. Some of the heat is reflected off Earth's surface.

18½ mph
(30 km/h) The average speed at which raindrops fall from the sky.

54,032°F
(30,000°C) The temperature of the air surrounding a bolt of lightning.

2,000
The average number of thunderstorms taking place on Earth every minute.

30
The number of storms recorded in the Atlantic Ocean in 2020–the highest ever.

Altostratus
Forming a thin sheet across the sky higher up in the atmosphere, these clouds bring light rain or sleet.

Nimbostratus
These dense, dark gray clouds usually bring heavy and long-lasting rain, followed by milder and drier weather.

Cirrus
These thin, wispy clouds form very high up in the sky and are made of ice crystals. They usually indicate pleasant, dry weather.

Lenticular
Wind passing over a hill sometimes sculpts rising air into these rare, lens-shaped clouds often mistaken for UFOs.

① This place in Death Valley is the hottest on Earth. In 1913, the temperature here reached 134°F (56.7°C)–the highest land temperature ever recorded.

More than 115,000 acres of the Angeles National Forest were destroyed by this event.

② Stretching from South Dakota to Texas, this region experiences around 1,000 "twisters" every year.

Wind speeds in a tornado can reach more than 310 mph (500 km/h).

③ While this state in the US faces similar blazes nearly every year, the ones that swept across it in 2020 were among its worst ever.

The massive storm that hit this Argentine city in 2017 was one of the heaviest ever, with raining pieces of ice as big as tennis balls.

The flooding from the storm left more than 1 million people homeless.

⑤ Wind speeds reached up to 174 mph (280 km/h) during this storm in 2005. The city of New Orleans was almost entirely flooded within a day.

⑥ With more than 40,000 strikes per night, the skies above Lake Maracaibo, Venezuela, provide a spectacular light show. This phenomenon is named after the river that empties in the lake.

Wild weather

Most of us only check out the weather when deciding what to wear for the day. However, in some parts of the world, weather can sometimes be extreme. From tornadoes and wildfires to hailstorms and floods, can you identify these wild weather phenomena?

⑦ This rare colored lightning, photographed here in Vivaro, Italy, occurs high above thunderstorms.

⑧ This Siberian town is the coldest inhabited place on Earth. In 1924, temperatures here fell to -91.2°F (-71.2°C).

Despite the water, street markets remained open and people still went to work.

⑩ In 1931, the worst rainstorm in history caused two rivers in China to overflow their banks. They flooded many major cities, including Nanjing and Wuhan.

One of the wettest places on Earth, this small town in eastern India is soaked by 467 in (11,872 cm) of rainfall every year.

The sand here is covered by a thin blanket of ice every 50 years or so.

⑪ In January 2021, an Algerian town in the Sahara Desert witnessed snowfall as the temperature plunged to -21°F (-3°C). This has only happened three times since 1979—the first time snow was recorded here.

An estimated 17 million tons of sand were carried by this storm into the city.

⑫ Often called "the red dawn," this event in 2009 blanketed cities including Canberra, Brisbane, and Sydney in a red haze.

TEST YOURSELF

STARTER	CHALLENGER	GENIUS!
California wildfires	Red sprites	Oymyakon winters
Yangtze-Huai flood	Hurricane Katrina	Aïn Sefra snowfall
Tornado Alley	Catatumbo lightning	Mawsynram monsoon
Eastern Australian dust storm	Furnace Creek	Córdoba hailstorm

NORTH AMERICA

North America

The landmass of North America tapers to the south and Central America, becoming the narrow land bridge to South America. To the east, the Caribbean Sea is speckled with hundreds of warm, tropical islands.

In numbers

 Population
600 million

 Size
9,233,255 sq miles
(24,230,000 sq km)

 Countries
23

At a glance

Discover some facts and stats about the continent of North America.

① Biggest country by area
Canada lies across the northern portion of the continent, occupying 3,855,100 sq miles (9,984,670 sq km).

② Smallest country by area
St. Kitts and Nevis are two tiny, paired Caribbean islands that total 100.8 sq miles (261 sq km), smaller than many cities.

③ Biggest city by population
Mexico City, Mexico, has 9.2 million residents in the city, and more than 21 million in the wider metropolitan area.

Fantastic festivals

From dazzling fireworks displays to lively street events, North America is filled with amazing celebrations.

Montreal Fireworks Festival
The world's biggest annual fireworks competition is held in La Ronde amusement park in Montreal, Canada, in front of 3 million spectators.

Day of the Dead
Families remember the dead in this Mexican holiday every November. Prayers, traditional foods, music, and dance are all prepared in honor of the deceased.

Junkanoo
In The Bahamas, this spectacular street parade of dance; music; and bright, elaborate costumes celebrates freedom from slavery. It occurs on Boxing Day and New Year's Day.

④ Biggest lake
Lake Superior in the US and Canada is 31,700 sq miles (82,097sq km). It is the most northern lake of the five Great Lakes.

⑤ Longest river
The Missouri River flows 2,341 miles (3,766 km) across the US, from the state of Montana to Mississippi.

⑥ Highest point
Denali—formerly known as Mt. McKinley—is in the state of Alaska and stands 20,310 ft (6,190 m) high.

⑦ Lowest point,
The Badwater Basin—large salt flats found in Death Valley in California lie 282 ft (86 m) below sea level.

I don't believe it

Because Mexico City, Mexico, is using up too much water from under the surface, it is sinking at an approximate rate of 20 in (50 cm) per year.

The Inuit

The Inuit are an Indigenous Arctic population who live in Alaska, Greenland, and the northern Canadian region of Nunavut, which means "our land" in the local language, Inuktitut. This Inuit Nunavut woman is shown in traditional handmade clothing. Hunting is at the core of their culture, and many people in the Nunavut community today still practice traditions that date back 5,000 years.

Liberty Island

Rising 305 ft (93 m) from ground level to torch, the iconic statue of the ancient Roman goddess of freedom, Libertas, stands on a small island in New York Bay. A gift from the people of France in 1884, the statue's torch lights the way to freedom.

More than 350 steps take visitors to the observation deck in the statue's crown.

How to cross the Panama Canal

A shortcut between the Atlantic and Pacific Oceans, the Panama Canal zigzags 51 miles (82 km) through the Central American country of Panama.

01. To use the canal, you need to pay a fee based on the size of your ship. There are also strict schedules, so don't be late!

02. Sets of canal locks (pictured) must be navigated. These locks raise the ship up to 85 ft (26 m) above sea level, allowing you to enter the canal.

03. Once on the canal, your ship travels through Gatun Lake, a large artificial lake that forms a major part of the canal.

04. At the end, a lock will lower you to ocean level. The journey typically takes 8–10 hours. Around 14,000 ships make the trip each year.

Countries of North America

Bordered by the Pacific and Atlantic Oceans, this continent boasts a diverse geography, from icy tundra to arid deserts and tropical rainforests. Its countries range from one of the most powerful nations on Earth to tiny island states with small populations in the thousands.

The world's largest island, Greenland, is in North America but is governed by Denmark, in Europe. About 80 percent of it is covered in ice, and the population is just under 60,000, mostly Greenlandic Inuit.

Greenland

Hudson Bay

1

2

The second largest country on Earth contains over 31,000 lakes and has the world's longest coastline. Two-fifths of its land is covered in forests.

This country is divided into 50 states, two of which—Hawaii and Alaska—do not share borders with the mainland. Alaska shares its border with western Canada, while Hawaii is a group of islands in the Pacific Ocean.

PACIFIC OCEAN

PACIFIC OCEAN

Hawaiian Islands

HAWAII (US)

3

Part of the former Aztec Empire, this country is known for its ancient ruins, such as Chichen Itza. Its landscape is dry and dusty, with vast deserts in the north, while the south is covered with lush rainforests.

THE CARIBBEAN

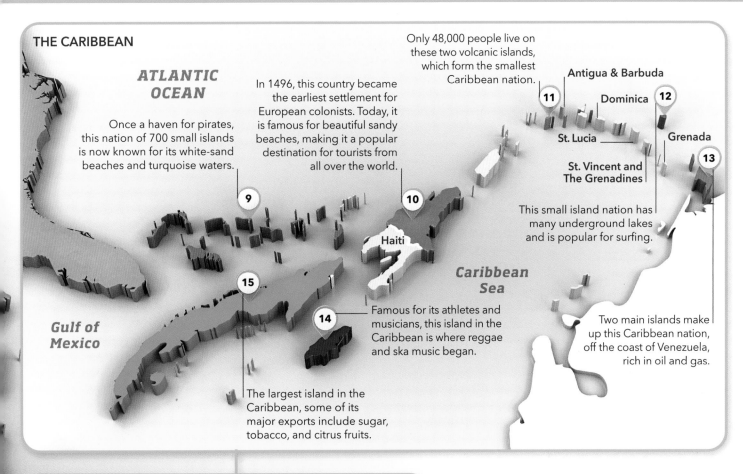

ATLANTIC OCEAN

Once a haven for pirates, this nation of 700 small islands is now known for its white-sand beaches and turquoise waters.

9

In 1496, this country became the earliest settlement for European colonists. Today, it is famous for beautiful sandy beaches, making it a popular destination for tourists from all over the world.

10

Only 48,000 people live on these two volcanic islands, which form the smallest Caribbean nation.

Antigua & Barbuda

11

Dominica

12

St. Lucia

Grenada

St. Vincent and The Grenadines

13

This small island nation has many underground lakes and is popular for surfing.

Haiti

Caribbean Sea

Gulf of Mexico

15

14

Famous for its athletes and musicians, this island in the Caribbean is where reggae and ska music began.

Two main islands make up this Caribbean nation, off the coast of Venezuela, rich in oil and gas.

The largest island in the Caribbean, some of its major exports include sugar, tobacco, and citrus fruits.

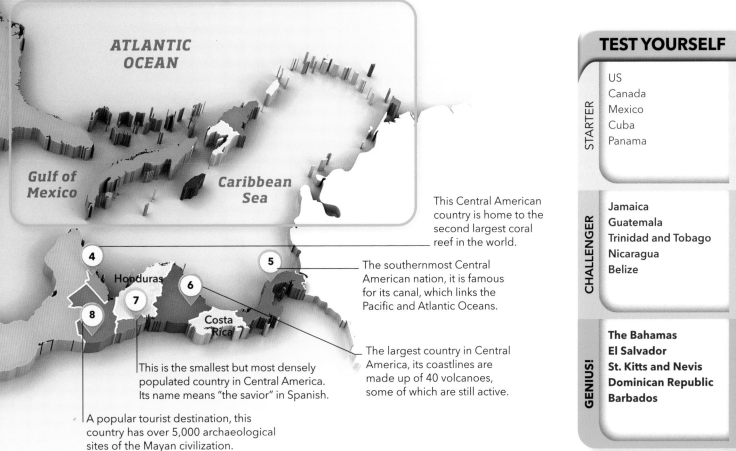

ATLANTIC OCEAN

Gulf of Mexico

Caribbean Sea

4

Honduras

5

6

7

8

Costa Rica

This Central American country is home to the second largest coral reef in the world.

The southernmost Central American nation, it is famous for its canal, which links the Pacific and Atlantic Oceans.

The largest country in Central America, its coastlines are made up of 40 volcanoes, some of which are still active.

This is the smallest but most densely populated country in Central America. Its name means "the savior" in Spanish.

A popular tourist destination, this country has over 5,000 archaeological sites of the Mayan civilization.

TEST YOURSELF

STARTER
US
Canada
Mexico
Cuba
Panama

CHALLENGER
Jamaica
Guatemala
Trinidad and Tobago
Nicaragua
Belize

GENIUS!
The Bahamas
El Salvador
St. Kitts and Nevis
Dominican Republic
Barbados

① Canada's fourth-largest city is the home of its national Parliament, which is located on the south bank of a major river with which it shares its name.

② More than one-sixth of Cuba's population lives in its colorful capital, the largest city in the Caribbean.

Canada

United States of America

HAWAII (USA)

Lights within this part of the Capitol Building's dome shine only when a law-making session is underway.

③ This city is named after the first US president and is home to the Capitol Building (pictured), where politicians debate and pass laws. The president lives in the White House nearby.

Mexico

The statue of the Greek goddess Nike is 22 ft (7 m) tall.

④ The Angel of Independence, commemorating the Mexican War of Independence, is one of the most recognizable landmarks of this city.

Capital cities

Usually, the capital of a country is its largest city, but not always. A government can also choose to make a different city the capital, or build a new one, as in the case of the US, which chose to build a new capital from scratch. With many located on the coasts, North America's capitals have often served as bustling trading hubs connecting the continent to the rest of the world.

(5) The capital of Haiti, on the Gulf of Gonâve, is a major Caribbean shipping and trading hub. Its pastel-colored houses cover the surrounding hills.

(6) Previously called Port Louis, the capital of Grenada is known for its horseshoe-shaped harbor, called the Carenage.

This life-size statue of Bob Marley was installed at the Trench Town Culture Yard Museum in 2015.

(7) The largest city in St. Lucia, its capital is built on land reclaimed from the sea. It is host to the annual St. Lucia Jazz and Arts festival.

The festival is visited by thousands of tourists every year.

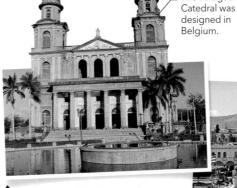

Dominica's capital was named by French settlers after a type of river grass.

(9) Backed by the Blue Mountains, the capital of Jamaica is the birthplace of the late legendary reggae singer Bob Marley.

TEST YOURSELF

STARTER
- Mexico City
- Washington DC
- Ottawa
- Havana
- San Salvador

CHALLENGER
- Kingston
- Castries
- Managua
- San José

GENIUS!
- **Port-au-Prince**
- **Tegucigalpa**
- **St. George's**
- **Roseau**
- **St. John's**

Antigua and Barbuda

The Bahamas

Cuba

Dominica
St. Lucia
Grenada

Dominican Republic

Haiti

Jamaica

Honduras

Belize

Nicaragua

Panama

El Salvador

Guatemala

Costa Rica

Flanked by mountains and the Caribbean Sea, the capital of Honduras started out as a gold and silver mining settlement.

Surrounded by rugged mountains, rainforests, and volcanoes, Costa Rica's bustling capital is also its largest city.

The Antigua Catedral was designed in Belgium.

(14) Founded in 1525, the oldest capital in Central America is found in El Salvador. The Plaza de Cagancha is an iconic landmark.

(12) Antigua's largest city, with a population of fewer than 25,000 inhabitants, is home to the scenic Redcliffe Quay promenade and waterfront.

(13) Named after the Aztec Nahuatl language phrase for "near water," Nicaragua's capital is home to the Antigua Catedral, which was nearly destroyed by an earthquake in 1972.

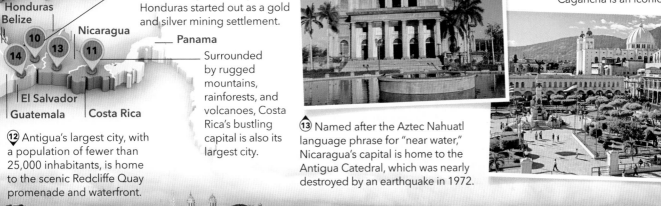

① The two triangles at the center of this flag represent the Pitons, a pair of volcanic mountains located in this island nation.

② The emblem on this country's flag shows an eagle perched on a cactus, eating a snake—an image associated with an Aztec legend.

The lake with an island represents the Aztec capital of Tenochtitlán.

③ First flown in 1974, this flag features seven stars and the spice nutmeg, which is one of this Caribbean nation's main exports.

④ Green, gold, and black symbolize agriculture, sunshine, and strength. It is the only flag in the world that does not have one of the colors red, white, or blue.

Raise the flag

Many of the colorful flags of the countries of North America include objects that represent the natural, geographical, or cultural heritage of the nation. They range from stars, stripes, and a maple leaf to an endangered parrot and even a nutmeg!

⑤ The white band on this flag signifies the snow that blankets the northern part of this large country every winter.

The maple leaf is the national emblem of this country.

⑥ Based on designs submitted by the people of the country, the yellow band on this flag represents the sandy beaches of this Caribbean island.

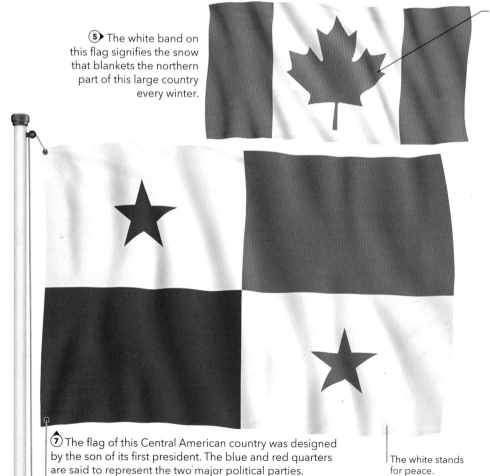

⑦ The flag of this Central American country was designed by the son of its first president. The blue and red quarters are said to represent the two major political parties.

The white stands for peace.

⑧ Designed by a school student, this flag belongs to a two-island nation. The diagonal black band symbolizes the African heritage of one of the islands.

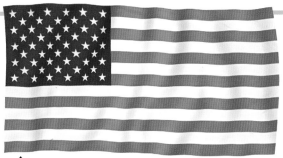

10 Symbols of this Central American country's logging industry make up the emblem on its flag. These include a mahogany tree and two men carrying tools.

The national motto, "I flourish in the shade," refers to the country's lush forests.

9 Known as the Stars and Stripes, this flag features a star for each of the country's 50 states and 13 stripes for the colonies that first formed the nation.

Green represents the lush vegetation of this island nation.

11 Only found in this nation, the rare Sisserou parrot featured on the flag is the country's national bird.

12 The blue stripes on this flag refer to the two bodies of water surrounding this Central American country—the Caribbean Sea and the Pacific Ocean.

TEST YOURSELF

13 This flag depicts the Sun rising against a black sky, which symbolizes the African heritage of the people of this Caribbean nation.

The triangle stands for equality.

14 This small Central American country has 20 volcanoes, five of which are represented on its flag's emblem.

① Around 76 miles (122 km) long and 7 miles (11 km) wide, this enormous mass of moving ice is the largest in North America. It lies on the border between Canada and Alaska.

Up to 350 ft (106 m) of the ice is above the water, while 250 ft (76 m) is submerged.

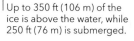

② This multicolored lake is found in Yellowstone National Park. It gets its colors from the bacteria that thrive in its scalding-hot water.

Greenland

Hudson Bay

③ Wind, rain, and ice have sculpted formations, known as hoodoos, at this national park in Utah.

The gorge has an average depth of 4,000 ft (1,220 m).

④ In one of the deepest river gorges in the world, the Colorado River has carved the majestic Horseshoe Bend.

PACIFIC OCEAN

⑤

HAWAII
(US)

⑤ On the island of Maui in Hawaii, one of the most dangerous wave systems in the world challenges surfers.

Natural wonders

Home to towering mountains, plummeting waterfalls, deep canyons, and astonishing rock formations, North America stretches from the Arctic in the north to just short of the equator in the south.

6 The 2,600-ft (792-m) wide Horseshoe Falls is the largest of three cascades that make up this spectacular natural formation on the US–Canada border.

The winding, slow-moving canals are home to alligators.

7 This network of swamps, tropical wetlands, and forests covers part of southern Florida. It provides habitats for around 350 bird species.

8 Also known as the Flowerpot Rocks, these unusual formations have been carved by waves from the Atlantic Ocean continuously lashing the coast.

TEST YOURSELF

STARTER
- Niagara Falls
- Grand Canyon
- The Pitons
- Grand Prismatic Spring

CHALLENGER
- Everglades
- Hubbard Glacier
- Nylon Pool
- Bryce Canyon

GENIUS!
- **Semuc Champey**
- **Hopewell Rocks**
- **Basaltic Prisms**
- **Jaws (Pe'ahi)**

ATLANTIC OCEAN

A sand formation just off the coast of Trinidad and Tobago has created a perfectly clear, protected pool in the middle of the ocean!

Gulf of Mexico

Caribbean Sea

10 These two volcanic peaks in Saint Lucia are more than 2,427 ft (740 m) tall.

Giant five- and six-sided columns of smooth rock line this spectacular ravine in Mexico. They were created by lava cooling very quickly.

11 The many tiers of this natural limestone bridge on the Cahabón River in Guatemala are known for their turquoise pools and tiny waterfalls.

① This river connects the Great Lakes with the Atlantic Ocean. It is home to many whale species, including minke and sperm whales.

Montreal's Biosphere Museum lies on the banks of this river.

② Only four bridges cross this 1,980-mile (3,190-km) long river, which runs through Canada and Alaska. It was the main means of transportation during the Klondike Gold Rush in the 19th century.

Bering Sea

Measuring 77 miles (124 km), this is the largest lake in Alaska. It is a popular spot for hikers and fishing enthusiasts.

This river flows through the Big Bend National Park.

HAWAII (USA)

PACIFIC OCEAN

④ More than 100 smaller rivers flow into this waterway, which starts in the Rocky Mountains and forms part of the US-Mexico border.

This lake holds almost 10 percent of the world's fresh water.

⑤ At 31,700 sq miles (82,100 sq km), the largest lake in North America is bigger than Panama. It is one of the five Great Lakes of North America.

The river has been an important trade route for centuries.

⑦ This iconic river is the longest in North America and runs through 10 states before emptying into the Gulf of Mexico.

⑥ Reaching a maximum depth of 1,950 ft (594 m), this is the deepest lake in the US. It was formed by the collapse of the Mount Mazama volcano 7,700 years ago.

The river runs through a lush tropical rainforest.

Rivers and lakes

While there are few rivers in the Caribbean Islands, the North American mainland has thousands. The US alone has over 250,000 rivers. A vital source of fresh water, they have also been used as crucial transportation and trade routes for centuries.

8 This river flows past the ancient Mayan city of Yaxchilan. It forms a part of the border between Guatemala and Mexico.

ATLANTIC OCEAN

Named after the US state in which it originates, this river runs through famous settlements such as Chattanooga and Scottsboro.

10 This Cuban river is the longest in the Caribbean. It is 229 miles (370 km) long; however, less than one-fifth of its length can be traveled by ships.

Gulf of Mexico

Caribbean Sea

This crater lake is located on the highest active volcano in Costa Rica.

12 This Costa Rican river features a 295-ft (90-m) tall waterfall and a scenic turquoise-colored pool surrounded by lush forest.

11 Rainwater running down the walls of this volcano collects minerals, which turn the water of this lake greenish yellow.

13 The largest freshwater lake in Central America is surrounded by volcanoes and is dotted with more than 400 islands.

Most volcanoes near this lake are constantly erupting.

TEST YOURSELF

STARTER	CHALLENGER	GENIUS!
Lake Superior	Rio Celeste	Usumacinta River
Mississippi River	Lake Nicaragua	Diego de la Haya
Rio Grande	Crater Lake	Yukon River
St. Lawrence River	Lake Iliamna	Rio Cauto
	Tennessee River	

55

① Known for its sightings of bears and bald eagles, this large area in the state of Alaska is mostly covered in rainforest.

② Canada's first national park contains the Rocky Mountains, Lake Louise, and more than 1,000 miles (1,600 km) of hiking trails.

This waterfall shares its name with the national park.

Engelmann spruce trees grow all over this national park.

③ The first protected area in the US is in California. It is home to many spectacular waterfalls and tall peaks such as Mount Lyell and El Capitan.

National parks

Conserving North America's natural beauty and biodiversity has become a priority in many nations. The US, for example, has 423 national parks and many other protected areas. Other countries also preserve portions of land and sea to protect the various species that live there.

④ Located above the continent's largest supervolcano, this is the first national park in the US. It contains many thermal springs and the well-known Old Faithful geyser.

Old Faithful is one of 500 active geysers in the park.

A protected marine park since 1995, these Mexican waters are home to the continent's oldest coral reefs.

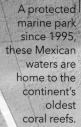

Hawaiian islands

⑥ Within these uninhabited Mexican islands lies a beach hidden in a crater. More than 800 species of fish and whales can be found in the surrounding waters.

This hidden beach is known as Playa Del Amor.

⑦ An abundance of wildlife, including moose and lynxes, can be found in this park on the island of Newfoundland.

Moose are a common sight here.

⑧ Named after the fog that covers its peaks and treetops, this popular park on the Tennessee–North Carolina border is the most visited in the US.

TEST YOURSELF

⑨ This park is a birdwatcher's paradise in The Bahamas, with mangrove trees, saltwater lakes, and dwarf rainforests that contain many rare bird species.

Lake Rosa is home to the world's largest breeding colony of American flamingos.

ATLANTIC OCEAN

PACIFIC OCEAN

⑩ Home to the Reich Falls, this rocky park in Jamaica gets its name from the mountain range that runs through it, as well as a common bird found there.

This protected area contains Panama's highest volcanic peak and more than 250 bird species.

Green sea turtles live and nest among the coral reefs here.

⑫ The protected waters of this park in the Caribbean Netherlands are home to more than 50 kinds of coral, 350 fish species, and some of the world's rarest turtles.

⑬ This Dominican national park takes its name from its three-peaked mountain. The park has areas of lush, dense rainforest as well as the Boiling Lake, which lies among its volcanic peaks.

Biomes

A biome is an area with a similar landscape, climate, animals, and plants. In North America, there are 13 biomes on land. They range from flooded grasslands teeming with bird life at Aransas National Wildlife Refuge; to cold, high-altitude Canadian boreal forests; and frozen regions like the Jakobshavn Glacier.

Types of biomes

- Tropical moist broadleaf forest
- Tropical dry broadleaf forest
- Tropical coniferous forest
- Temperate broadleaf forest
- Temperate coniferous forest
- Tropical grassland and savanna
- Desert and dry shrubland
- Temperate grassland and savanna
- Flooded grassland and savanna
- Mediterranean forest and woodland
- Boreal forest
- Tundra
- Ice

Biomes of North America

Nebraska Sand Hills
Around 700 plant species bloom in this mostly untouched temperate grassland growing on sand dunes.

Canadian boreal forests
Showing little sign of human impact and teeming with animals and plants, this forest covers 1.04 million sq miles (2.7 million sq km).

Humboldt State Park
These large, temperate coniferous forests contain massive redwood trees, some of which are more than 2,000 years old.

California chapparal
Dry scrubland and Mediterranean forests grow on the shallow soils here, including many drought-resistant plants, from sage to cacti.

Death Valley
One of the driest places on Earth, temperatures here soar above 122°F (50°C) in summer.

Sierra Madre del Sur
Extending 620 miles (1,000 km), this mountain range is covered in tropical coniferous forests.

Balsas dry forests
Pine and oak trees thrive in this Mexican tropical dry broadleaf forest, where valleys rise up to 656 ft (200 m).

I don't believe it !

Costa Rica covers 0.03 percent of Earth's land surface yet contains 6 percent of the species of all animals and plants.

Pacific Ocean kelp forest

Some seaweeds form large, dense underwater forests, providing food and habitats for many marine plants and animals. This Pacific Ocean kelp forest on the coast of Anacapa Island, US, is home to more than 1,000 species of sea life, including California sea lions.

Jakobshavn Glacier
Producing 4.4 billion tons of icebergs a year, this glacier in Greenland is 1 mile (1.6 km) thick.

Auyuittuq National Park
Rocky mountains, glaciers, and Arctic tundra with low-growing plants are found in this northern part of Canada.

Adirondack Mountains
Cool in winter, this 9,375-sq-mile (24,281-sq-km) temperate broadleaf forest is the largest in the world.

Aransas National Wildlife Refuge
This area of Texas known for its water birds is mostly subtropical grasslands, marshes, and lakes.

Everglades National Park
This massive flooded grassland is home to leatherback turtles and Florida panthers.

Hispaniolan moist forests
Stunning waterfalls are found in this tropical broadleaf forest covering 17,761 sq miles (46,000 sq km).

Conservation facts

🍃 With the end of mass logging in Costa Rica (pictured), more than half of the country is forested today.

🍃 Half of the coral in the Caribbean reefs has died in 50 years, much of it due to climate change.

🍃 Thanks to a breeding program, in 2019, 4,000 once-thought extinct Bermuda land snails were released into the wild.

In numbers

800,000
The total population of black bears across North America.

62%
The percentage of the world's lakes found in Canada.

432
The number of national parks located in North America.

① This Costa Rican butterfly is named after the color of its wings, which is similar to that of a green mineral.

② Diving at speeds of up to 100 mph (160 km/h) to snatch up fish or snakes, this powerful bird of prey is the national emblem of the US.

It has a wingspan of up to 8 ft (2.5 m).

③ An excellent climber, this large mammal uses its short claws to scramble up trees and feast on berries, buds, nuts, insects, and honey.

Amazing animals

④ This is one of the largest and noisiest monkeys in Central America. It is named after the loud cries made by males to mark their territory.

More than 450 mammal, 500 reptile, and 2,000 bird species thrive across a wide range of North American habitats—from cold boreal forests in northern Canada and the US to the tropical rainforests of the Caribbean.

⑥ The national bird of Trinidad and Tobago uses its long, curved bill to probe for food in soft mud.

Its flat shell helps it glide through water.

⑤ Every winter, millions of these brightly colored insects fly thousands of miles south from southern Canada and the US to Mexico in search of warmth and food.

Substances in the shrimps and other shellfish it eats turn its plumage red.

⑦ Found in slow-moving rivers or lakes, this animal gets its name from the patterns formed by lines on its skin and shell.

8 This is the national bird of Guatemala. It nests high up in rainforest trees, rarely visiting the ground.

It has dazzling red and green feathers.

A long, flexible snout helps it probe for insects in narrow crevices.

9 Only found in a few lakes in Mexico, this creature has feathery external gills for breathing under water.

10 This nocturnal insect eater found in Haiti and the Dominican Republic has a venomous bite, which it uses to defend itself.

11 Named after the light-colored fur above its neck, this clever tropical monkey uses sticks and stones as tools to obtain food.

Males have very long tail streamers.

A wormlike part of its tongue lures fish closer before it clamps down on them.

12 The largest lizard in the US can grow up to 22 in (56 cm) long. Highly venomous, it overpowers its prey with multiple bites.

The bold pattern warns predators to stay away.

14 The largest rodent in North America, this animal creates a protective moat around its home by building dams across forest streams.

Powerful jaws are used to snap up salmon swimming up a river or stream.

13 Found in southeastern US, this pond dweller has a ridged shell that helps it blend into swampy vegetation.

15 Up to 10 ft (3 m) tall when standing on its hind legs, this powerful mammal is named after its silver-tipped fur.

Its webbed rear feet help it steer while swimming.

TEST YOURSELF

STARTER	CHALLENGER	GENIUS!
North American beaver	**Monarch butterfly**	**Gila monster**
Bald eagle	**Alligator snapping turtle**	**Hispaniolan solenodon**
Grizzly bear	**Malachite butterfly**	**Axolotl**
Scarlet ibis	**Northern map turtle**	**Resplendent quetzal**
American black bear	**Panamanian white-faced capuchin**	**Mantled howler**

① This artificial waterway, 51 miles (82 km) long, opened in 1914 after a long and difficult construction project.

② This gigantic 19th-century stone fortress, featuring 365 cannons and 132-ft (40-m) high walls, was built in Haiti to prevent foreign invasions.

Around 14,000 ships use this shortcut between the Atlantic and Pacific Oceans every year.

③ This enormous barrier across the Colorado River is 60 stories high and generates enough electricity for 1.3 million homes.

Human-made wonders

This was the world's tallest building for more than 40 years.

North America is home to many impressive buildings, bridges, and towering structures—both old and new. From the mighty monuments of the past to modern marvels of engineering, art, and design, cool constructions are found in every corner of the continent.

④ Hidden within the lush Guatemalan rainforest, this ancient Mayan city was discovered in the 1840s and contains several limestone pyramids and temples.

This temple has a total of 365 steps, one for each day of a solar year.

⑤ New York City's most famous building is a 102-story skyscraper with 73 elevators. It was completed in 1931 in only 410 days.

7▶ Home to Ancestral Puebloans more than 700 years ago, this 150-room structure is the largest cliff dwelling in North America and forms part of a key Colorado attraction.

During the 1200s, this palace had almost 100 residents.

6▶ This iconic suspension bridge opened in 1937 and stretches 4,200 ft (1,280 m). It connects San Francisco to Marin County.

This is the most photographed hotel in the world.

The giant roller coaster is 456 ft (139 m) high.

8▶ The world's tallest and fastest roller coaster is in the US. It catapults its riders as high as a 45-story building in a few seconds.

9▶ Opened in 1893 to serve the Canadian-Pacific railroad, this 611-room grand hotel has 18 floors and towers over Old Québec.

Each president's head is approximately 60 ft (18.3 m) tall and 17.8 ft (5.4 m) wide.

The SkyPod observation deck offers stunning views of Toronto.

10◀ Canada's 1,815-ft (553-m) high communications mast is the tallest structure in North America.

11▶ More than 440,000 tons of rock was blasted to produce the giant sculptures of four US presidents: George Washington, Thomas Jefferson, Theodore Roosevelt, and Abraham Lincoln.

12▶ This ancient Mayan city in Mexico contains many pyramids and stone-carved buildings, all linked by more than 80 pathways.

TEST YOURSELF

STARTER
Empire State Building
Golden Gate Bridge
Mount Rushmore
Panama Canal

CHALLENGER
Mesa Verde
CN Tower
Hoover Dam
Kingda Ka

GENIUS!
Château Frontenac
Chichén Itzá
Citadelle Laferrière
Tikal

SOUTH AMERICA

South America

Although large in area, South America has the fewest countries of all habitable continents. Home to the world's largest rainforest, the Amazon, and the longest mountain range, the Andes, South America is also rich in music and dance.

In numbers

Population
420 million

Size
6,890,000 sq miles
(17,840,000 sq km)

Countries
12

At a glance

Discover some facts and stats about the continent of South America.

(1) Biggest country by area
Brazil is by far the biggest country in South America, with an area of 3.29 million sq miles (8.52 million sq km).

(2) Smallest country by area
Suriname, a tropical nation located on the northeastern coast of the continent, has an area of 63,235 sq miles (163,820 sq km).

(3) Biggest city by population
São Paulo, Brazil, has 12.2 million residents in the city, and more than 21 million in the wider metropolitan area.

(4) Biggest lake
Lake Titicaca sits on the border between Bolivia and Peru. It has a surface area of 3,220 sq miles (8,340 sq km).

(5) Longest river
The Amazon River flows through Brazil, Colombia, and Peru. It is 4,345 miles (6,992 km) long.

(6) Highest point
Aconcagua, in the Andes Mountains of Argentina, stands 22,831 ft (6,959 m) above sea level.

(7) Lowest point
Laguna del Carbon in Argentina is 344 ft (104.9 m) below sea level. Several dinosaur fossils have been found here.

Fantastic festivals

Many festivals are held in South America. People dance for days, mark the new year, and even lasso steers.

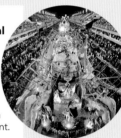

Carnival
With millions of people taking to the streets alongside elaborate floats, the Carnival in Rio de Janeiro, Brazil, occurs annually in the lead up to the Christian season of Lent.

Inti Raymi
Peru's Sun Festival happens on the shortest day every year. It marks the start of the Incan new year and draws in thousands of visitors to the ancient Inca capital of Cusco.

Gaucho Festival
This energetic and exciting event turns the small Argentinian town of San Antonio de Areco into a week-long celebration of South American cowboys, known as gauchos.

I don't believe it

One-third of the entire landmass of South America is covered by the Amazon Rainforest.

How to dance the tango

For the ultimate tango lesson, go to Argentina and the back streets of Buenos Aires, where the dance began and is still danced today.

01. Find a partner—this is a dance for two people. Traditionally, the man leads the woman, holding her close as she follows his steps.

02. Listen to the music—this tells the story of the dance. It's usually a sad and dramatic tale of broken hearts and the struggle of two lovers to be together.

03. The lead dancer then takes their partner in an embrace and, as the music plays, he chooses the steps and together they interpret the music. No two tangos are ever the same.

The Kayapó

In Brazil, the Indigenous Kayapó people are impacted by companies causing deforestation and pollution where they live. Chief Raoni is an environmental activist who promotes the plight of the Kayapó people. He is pictured in Brussels, Belgium, on a climate change march.

Galápagos Islands

Although part of Ecuador, the Galápagos Islands lie around 600 miles (965 km) from the Ecuadorian coast. Many animals and plants here are not found anywhere else in the world, from giant tortoises to daisy trees. The marine iguanas here are the only lizards in the world that forage for food—mostly algae—in the ocean.

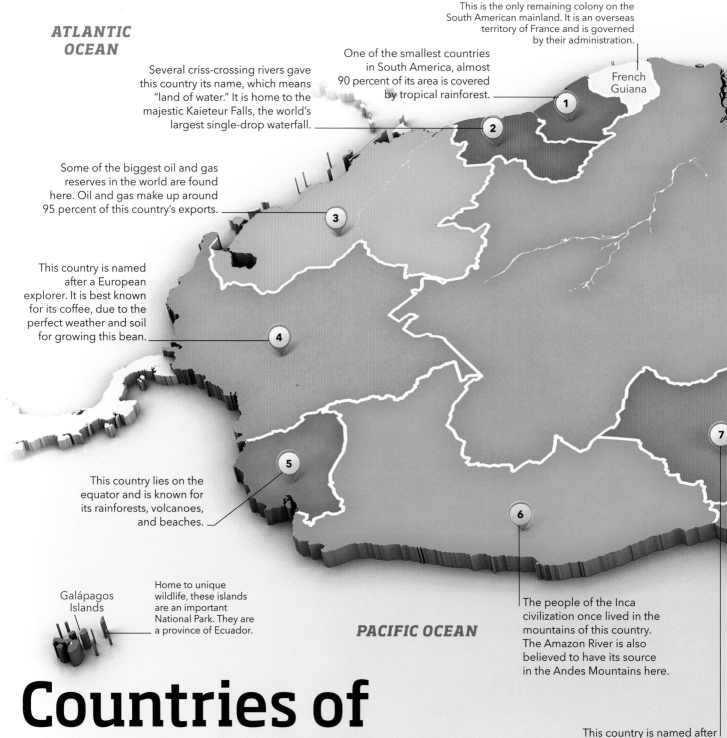

ATLANTIC OCEAN

Several criss-crossing rivers gave this country its name, which means "land of water." It is home to the majestic Kaieteur Falls, the world's largest single-drop waterfall.

One of the smallest countries in South America, almost 90 percent of its area is covered by tropical rainforest.

This is the only remaining colony on the South American mainland. It is an overseas territory of France and is governed by their administration.

French Guiana

Some of the biggest oil and gas reserves in the world are found here. Oil and gas make up around 95 percent of this country's exports.

This country is named after a European explorer. It is best known for its coffee, due to the perfect weather and soil for growing this bean.

This country lies on the equator and is known for its rainforests, volcanoes, and beaches.

Galápagos Islands

Home to unique wildlife, these islands are an important National Park. They are a province of Ecuador.

PACIFIC OCEAN

The people of the Inca civilization once lived in the mountains of this country. The Amazon River is also believed to have its source in the Andes Mountains here.

This country is named after one of South America's military and political leaders who fought for independence over European colonial rule. Much of this country lies on a high plateau, called the Altiplano.

Countries of South America

Until the 1800s, most of the countries of South America were under Spanish and Portuguese rule. Today, this continent has 12 independent countries, but the impact of the past rulers can be seen in their languages and cultures.

ANSWERS: 1. Suriname 2. Guyana 3. Venezuela 4. Colombia 5. Ecuador 6. Peru 7. Bolivia 8. Brazil 9. Paraguay 10. Uruguay 11. Argentina 12. Chile

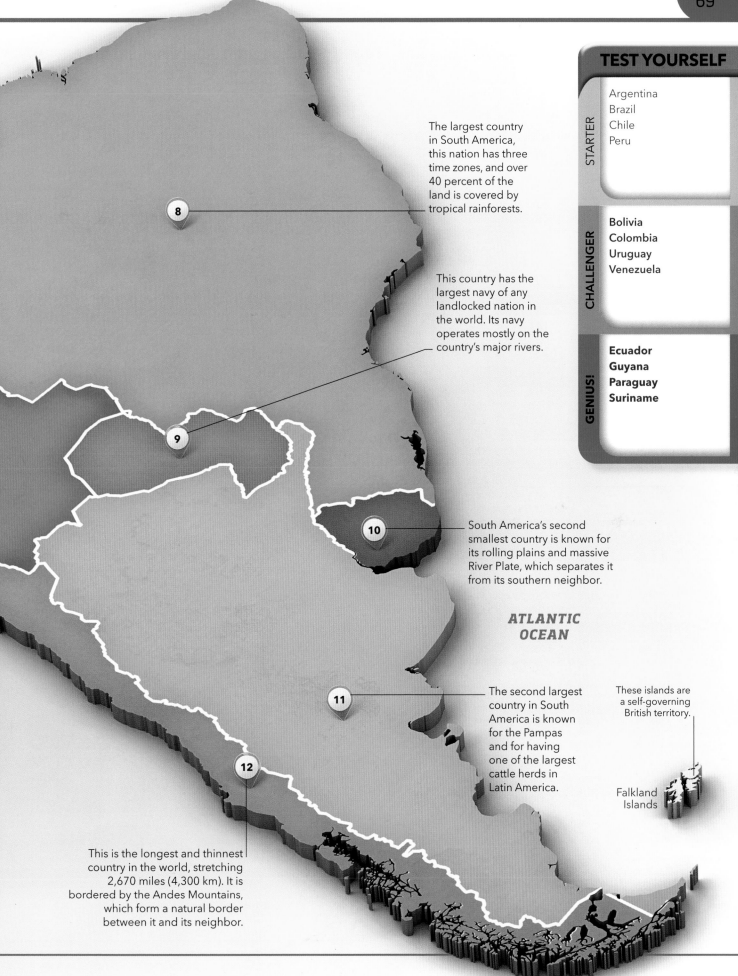

The largest country in South America, this nation has three time zones, and over 40 percent of the land is covered by tropical rainforests.

8

This country has the largest navy of any landlocked nation in the world. Its navy operates mostly on the country's major rivers.

9

South America's second smallest country is known for its rolling plains and massive River Plate, which separates it from its southern neighbor.

10

ATLANTIC OCEAN

The second largest country in South America is known for the Pampas and for having one of the largest cattle herds in Latin America.

11

These islands are a self-governing British territory.

Falkland Islands

This is the longest and thinnest country in the world, stretching 2,670 miles (4,300 km). It is bordered by the Andes Mountains, which form a natural border between it and its neighbor.

12

TEST YOURSELF

STARTER
Argentina
Brazil
Chile
Peru

CHALLENGER
Bolivia
Colombia
Uruguay
Venezuela

GENIUS!
Ecuador
Guyana
Paraguay
Suriname

Capital cities

South America has 12 countries but 13 capital cities—Bolivia has two capitals. Many of these cities date back hundreds of years and trace their roots to Indigenous communities and medieval empires, while some have a uniquely modern story to tell—one of them was built from scratch only 60 years ago! Can you identify them all?

1 This city was built where the Suriname River meets the Atlantic Ocean. The grand Presidential Palace, which houses the head of state, is also located here.

2 Revolutionary leader Simón Bolívar was born in the capital of Venezuela. The Paseo Los Próceres monument includes a statue honoring him.

Pichincha, an active volcano, regularly spews ash over the capital of Ecuador, which is also the oldest capital city in South America.

Galápagos Islands

4 The Wakili Totem Pole in the capital of Guyana celebrates the Indigenous people's abiding respect of the forest and all that it provides.

This 20-ft (6-m) high sculpture was carved by local artist Oswald Hussein from the Lokono Indigenous community.

5 This capital city is located between the Sechura Desert and the Pacific Ocean. The Miraflores district, the city's commercial hub, lies along the seafront.

The government of Bolivia is based in this city, which is also the world's highest capital. It is located 11,975 ft (3,650 m) above sea level.

This capital is known as the "white city" after the color of most of its buildings.

7 Nestled in the northern Andes Mountains, Colombia's capital city is famous for its music and coffee.

Visitors can take a cable car to the top of Monserrate, a hill in the middle of this city.

8 This city is the judicial capital of Bolivia—the Supreme Court of Justice is located here. It was named after an iconic South American revolutionary leader.

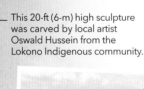

Map labels: Suriname, Guyana, Venezuela, Colombia, Ecuador, Peru, Bolivia

The bell tower is 66 ft (22 m) tall and has four bells.

9 Designed and built in 1960, Brazil's capital city is known for its unique buildings, such as this cathedral.

10 Some of South America's most important soccer matches are hosted at the Defensores del Chaco Stadium in Paraguay's capital city.

The Pocitos is one of the city's most popular beaches.

Brazil

9

10
Paraguay

Uruguay

12 **11**

13
Argentina

Chile

Falkland Islands

11 Located on the banks of the Rio de la Plata, the capital of Uruguay is home to several stunning river beaches.

12 A lively hub of art, music, dance, and soccer, this city is home to many colorful neighborhoods and is the birthplace of the tango.

The district of La Boca is known for its brightly colored buildings.

With a height of 986 ft (300 m), the Gran Torre is South America's tallest building.

13 Surrounded by the Andes Mountains, the capital of Chile is the most densely populated city in South America.

2 The red and white on this flag are the colors of the Inca Empire, which traces its origin to this country.

The coat of arms includes this country's national animal, the vicuña—a mammal related to the camel.

1 The Sun of May in the center of this flag represents the dawn of a new era. The colors were derived from the flag flown by revolutionary leader Manuel Belgrano.

Red stands for valor.

Raise the flag

South America has a diverse assortment of flags, but many countries often share symbols, such as the Sun or stars. The colors or patterns can represent different things, including famous natural landmarks or the number of provinces in a country. Some flags show an emblem or a coat of arms reflecting iconic national features. How many flags can you identify?

3 The 27 stars on the flag of this soccer-loving nation, known for the Amazon rainforest, represent the 26 states and one capital district in the country.

4 The colors of this flag were inspired by the French Revolution. Unusually, it has a different symbol on each side—a star on the front and a lion on the back.

5 Yellow, blue, and red were the colors of revolutionary leader Francisco de Miranda. The Andean condor, featured on the coat of arms, is the national bird of this country.

The coat of arms also depicts the Guayas River, with Mount Chimborazo behind it.

ANSWERS: 1. Argentina 2. Peru 3. Brazil 4. Paraguay 5. Ecuador 6. Chile 7. Colombia 8. Bolivia 9. Venezuela 10. Guyana 11. Uruguay 12. Suriname

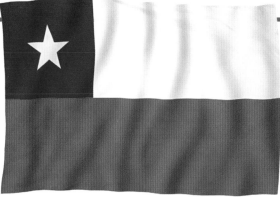

This flag was inspired by the flags of rebels who secured the country's independence from Spain.

(6) The white stripe at the top of this US-inspired flag stands for the Andes, the mountain range that runs the full length of this long, thin country.

(7) Striped and striking, this three-colored flag represents the country's gold, the ocean, and courage.

(8) The yellow band on this flag, which belongs to the country originally known as Upper Peru, represents the nation's rich mineral reserves.

The blue band represents independence.

(9) The eight stars across the center of the flag represent the eight provinces of this country, which is home to the Angel Falls—the world's tallest waterfall.

(10) This flag is also known as the "Golden Arrow" because of the arrowhead depicted on it, which is symbolic of the country's bright future.

TEST YOURSELF

STARTER
Brazil
Argentina
Peru
Colombia

CHALLENGER
Venezuela
Bolivia
Ecuador
Chile

GENIUS!
Paraguay
Uruguay
Guyana
Suriname

White and light blue were the colors of the badges worn by revolutionaries during the 1800s.

(12) The flag of South America's smallest country was chosen from designs sent in by the public. The star at the center is a symbol of hope and unity.

(11) Inspired by the flag of a neighboring country, the nine bands on this flag represent the country's nine original regions. The flag was created by revolutionary leader José Artigas.

1 With a height of 979 m (3,212 ft), this cascade in Venezuela is the tallest in the world. It is twice as high as the Empire State Building in New York!

2 The highest table-top mountain in South America, a feature also known as a tepui, is 9,219 ft (2,810 m) tall.

Caribbean Sea

3 The symmetrical slopes of this snow-topped active volcano attract many hikers. At 19,393 ft (5,911m) tall, it is Ecuador's second-highest peak.

PACIFIC OCEAN

TEST YOURSELF

STARTER
Perito Moreno Glacier
Sugarloaf Mountain
Iguazu Falls
Salar de Uyuni

CHALLENGER
Angel Falls
Cotapaxi
Valle de la Luna
Mount Roraima
Colca Canyon

GENIUS!
Paracas National Reserve
Torres del Paine National Park
The Pantanal

This coastal desert in Peru is home to seals, flamingos, and Humboldt penguins.

The valleys of this gorge in Peru are 11,155 ft (3,400 m) deep, almost twice that of the Grand Canyon!

6 Extending for 4,050 sq miles (10,490 sq km), the world's largest salt flats cover an area four times larger than Luxembourg. They are the remains of ancient lakes that dried up, leaving behind a thick crust of salt.

Natural wonders

South America's diverse landscapes include bone-dry deserts, giant winding rivers, icy glaciers, spectacular waterfalls, high-altitude plains, and lush green wetlands. Here are just a few of these natural marvels—do you know which is which?

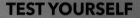

7 The world's largest inland wetland covers parts of Brazil, Bolivia, and Paraguay. It is full of exotic wildlife, from giant anteaters to river otters.

ATLANTIC OCEAN

8 At 1,300 ft (396 m) high, this sweetly named peak towers over Rio de Janeiro in Brazil. Visitors can reach it by cable car to admire the view.

9 Around 275 separate falls form a massive 1.7-mile (2.7-km) long horseshoe of plunging water on the border of Brazil and Argentina.

12 Wind and water erosion have shaped the rocks in this part of Chile's Atacama Desert into a Moon-like landscape.

10 This protected wilderness area in the extreme south of Chile is known for its towering granite peaks, forests, and crystal-clear lakes.

ATLANTIC OCEAN

11 This mass of ice moves forward by around 6½ ft (2 m) every day. It is the third-largest store of fresh water on Earth.

Rivers and lakes

The Amazon might be South America's most famous river, but the continent is also home to many other stunning waterways and lakes, some of which are colored brightly by salts, minerals, and algae in the water. Can you identify them all?

The Peñol Rock is around 722 ft (220 m) tall.

① This Colombian lake is dotted with green islands, one of which is home to the massive Peñol Rock.

ATLANTIC OCEAN

Volcanic minerals give the water its green color.

South America's second-longest river flows through Venezuela. An endangered species of crocodile found in its basin is named after it.

③ Located in Ecuador, this caldera lake, which formed when water filled the crater of a dormant volcano, is 820 ft (250 m) deep.

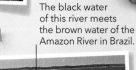

The black water of this river meets the brown water of the Amazon River in Brazil.

⑤ With a 165-ft (50-m) deep main channel that winds through the world's largest rainforest, this is the biggest river in the world by volume.

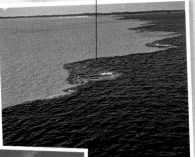

④ A type of acid released by decaying vegetation along its banks gives this river the black color after which it is named.

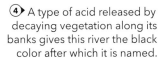

Moriche palm trees grow along the banks of this lake.

⑥ This tree-lined Peruvian lake, created by the Madre de Dios River, is home to giant otters and more than 6,500 species of fish.

⑦ South America's largest lake lies on the border of Peru and Bolivia. It is home to the floating Uros Islands, which were built using totora reeds.

8 Also called the Red Lake, this shallow saltwater lake in Bolivia gets its color from a type of algae that grows in it.

Flamingos flock to this lake during summer to feast on plankton.

9 Named after its bright green water that is rich in minerals, this Bolivian lake is located near the border of Chile, within the Eduardo Avaroa National Reserve.

The dry landscape of the Altiplano surrounds this lake.

10 Rapids, waterfalls, and canyons—such as the Xingó Canyon in Brazil—are common sights on the upper stretches of this river.

Named after one of the countries it flows through, this river feeds the Pantanal—the world's largest tropical wetland.

12 This river marks the border between Paraguay and Brazil. Its name means "as big as the sea."

13 This striking turquoise lake, fed by the Paine River, is located in Chile's Torres del Paine National Park.

Guanacos can be seen on the banks of this lake.

Mount Tronador, an extinct volcano, stands on one side of this lake.

PACIFIC OCEAN

The General Artigas Bridge joins Argentina and Uruguay.

15 Five international bridges cross this river, which is named after one of the countries through which it flows.

14 Located within a national park, this lake in Argentina is more than 1,400 ft (425 m) deep.

① Once dried and roasted, the berries of this plant are used to make one of the world's most popular hot drinks.

Grape-sized berries grow in clusters on the branches.

Long, clawed fingers help to dig out insects from tree barks.

The long tail helps it grip branches as it jumps from tree to tree.

② These trees have long, branching roots that anchor them to the wet, waterlogged soil along the edges of water courses.

The dense network of roots helps prevent soil erosion by slowing down the flow of water.

③ Named after the color of its fur, this small primate is endangered due to deforestation and poaching.

④ This plant is found high up on rainforest tree trunks and branches. Its large, waxy leaves hold tiny pools of water, with flowers in their center.

Frogs lay their eggs in the pool.

⑤ This sharp-toothed hunter is the biggest predator in the Amazon. Its dark scales help camouflage it at night.

This creature has up to 76 teeth that are used to grab prey.

The sap is extracted by cutting grooves into its bark.

⑥ This tree oozes a milky sap called latex, which can be used to make tires, toys, shoes, and more.

This bird can be identified easily by its blue facial skin.

⑦ This plant eater is also known as the stinkbird because of its foul smell. Its chicks have claws on their wings, which they use to climb through branches.

TEST YOURSELF

STARTER	CHALLENGER	GENIUS!
Black caiman	**Bald uakari**	**Anavilhanas archipelago**
Golden lion tamarin	**Giant water lily**	**Bromeliad**
Coffee tree	**Guianan Cock-of-the-rock**	**Hoatzin**
Cacao tree	**Rubber trees**	**Kapok tree**
Mangrove tree		

8 The brightly colored males of this species of bird are known for their elaborate dance on the forest floor to attract females.

Males and females have a half-moon crest on the head that even covers the bill.

9 The seed of this plant is the most important ingredient in chocolate.

The seeds are found inside large pods.

10 This Amazonian monkey is easily identified by its red face and bare head.

The striking color is caused by blood flow beneath the skin.

Large buttress roots help support the tree's weight.

11 Growing high into the rainforest canopy, this tree can grow 230 ft (70 m) tall. It has a spiny bark, which prevents animals from chewing it.

The 400 islands are covered by forests.

12 Upstream from Manaus, Brazil, is the world's largest group of river islands.

The mammal uses its tail to stay balanced while walking on branches.

The Amazon

Extending over 2.7 million sq miles (7 million sq km), the basin of the Amazon River covers an area that is almost the size of Australia! Within it lies one of our planet's most diverse habitats: the Amazon rainforest. One in 10 of the world's plant and animal species are found here.

13 Floating on top of the water, the huge leaves of this plant can span 9.8 ft (3 m) across.

The flower blooms only for a few days during summer.

ANSWERS: 1. Coffee tree 2. Mangrove tree 3. Golden lion tamarin 4. Bromeliad 5. Black caiman 6. Rubber trees 7. Hoatzin 8. Guianan Cock-of-the-rock 9. Cacao tree 10. Bald uakari 11. Kapok tree 12. Anavilhanas archipelago 13. Giant water lily

Biomes

In South America, there are nine land biomes—areas with a similar landscape, climate, animals, and plants. They include tropical broadleaf forests such as the lush-green Amazon; deserts like the Atacama; and wide, flat grasslands and savanna found in the south of the continent.

In numbers

97%
The percentage of the Galápagos Islands that is designated as a national park.

1,700
The number of bird species in the Andes Mountains.

2.5 million
The number of known insect species that live in the Amazon Rainforest.

Coastal Patagonia

The waters off the eastern coast of Argentina are home to four types of whales—including the southern right whale (pictured)—seals, dolphins, sea otters, penguins, and many species of fish.

Conservation facts

Invasive species, such as fire ants, are a threat to the Galápagos Islands (pictured). Removing them is vital to the survival of native species.

Today, conservationists are protecting animal habitats in the heavily deforested Atlantic Forests in Brazil and Paraguay.

Amazon ecotourism gives jobs to local people while ensuring small groups visit protected areas.

Biomes of South America

Gran Sabana
Home to an impressive variety of flora and fauna, this Venezuelan region includes tropical grasslands dotted with lakes and valleys.

Huascaran National Park
Lake Parón is one feature of this park in Peru, which also contains Cordillera Blanca, the world's highest tropical mountain range.

Atacama Desert
The Valley of the Moon is a stony, sandy area in this vast Chilean desert, some parts of which have had no rain for 20 million years.

Elqui Valley
In the southern reaches of the Atacama Desert, this area of Chile has a Mediterranean climate. It is a well-known wine-making region.

Types of biomes

- Tropical moist broadleaf forest
- Temperate broadleaf forest
- Desert and dry shrubland
- Flooded grassland and savanna
- Mountain grassland
- Tropical dry broadleaf forest
- Tropical grassland and savanna
- Temperate grassland and savanna
- Mediterranean forest and woodland

Amazon Rainforest
Competing for light above the canopy, trees here grow very tall in warm, wet conditions. Sadly, deforestation continues to be a major problem here.

Pantanal Matogrossense National Park
Water lilies float in the flooded grasslands of this Brazilian park. It is a haven for all sorts of wildlife, from river otters to jaguars.

Torotoro National Park
Tropical dry forests are found in this small national park in Bolivia. Thousands of fossilized dinosaur footprints have been found here.

The Pampas
Dotted with giant pampas grasses that can grow up to 12 ft (3.6 m) tall, these flat grasslands in Argentina cover around 295,000 sq miles (760,000 sq km). Cattle can be seen grazing in this region.

Oncol Park
This coastal park in Chile overlooks the Pacific Ocean. Covered in broadleaf temperate rainforest, this region is home to Andean foxes and cougars.

Animal life

South American wildlife ranges from sluggish tree dwellers to high-flying birds. Here are four animals that live in different habitats.

Ecuadorian hillstar
Moving constantly to keep warm, this tiny hummingbird lives in the Andes Mountains at altitudes up to 11,500 ft (5,200 m). Habitats include grasslands, shrubland, and wooded areas.

Brown-throated sloth
This slow-moving mammal lives in the tropical forests throughout the continent and can sleep for up to 18 hours a day! It has long, curved claws for gripping onto tree branches.

Guanaco
Related to camels, the guanaco lives in dry, open country in the mountains, mostly in Argentina. It does not need to drink, getting all the water it needs from the plants it eats.

Toco toucan
This tropical bird is famous for its long beak, perfect for plucking fruit out of reach on branches too thin to stand on. It spends most of its time high up in the canopy of South American forests, such as the Amazon.

I don't believe it

In a dense rainforest, it can take a raindrop 10 minutes to drip from the top of the trees to the forest floor.

2 Weighing up to 550 lb (250 kg), this enormous reptile is the heaviest snake in the world. It squeezes prey to death with its powerful muscles.

Blotchy markings give camouflage in muddy rivers.

1 Often heard chattering high up in the rainforest canopy, this little animal springs through the trees in search of fruit and insects.

A long tail helps this animal keep its balance.

Its small ears can fold back to keep water out when the animal is swimming.

3 This pig-sized animal is actually the world's largest rodent. It lives in herds near rivers and swamps and is a strong swimmer.

A "pit" below each eye has glands that can sense the body heat of nearby prey.

4 Bright green and venomous, this tree-living snake can be found in the world's largest rainforest. It is also known as the green jararaca.

5 Only found on one group of islands, this slow-moving animal can live for more than 100 years. It can grow to 4 ft (1.2 m) long.

Amazing animals

There are a huge range of habitats in South America, including rainforests, deserts, and grasslands. Each of these is home to animals that are perfectly adapted to their environment. This makes for a continent with a rich variety of curious creatures, from toxic frogs to giant tortoises. Can you identify them all?

6 Bright colors warn predators that this animal's skin is highly toxic. It lives in tiny pools of water in leaves, high up in the rainforest.

ANSWERS: 1. Common squirrel monkey 2. Green anaconda 3. Capybara 4. Amazonian palm viper 5. Galápagos giant tortoise 6. Red poison dart frog 7. Red-footed tortoise 8. Giant leaf frog 9. Pale-throated sloth 10. Amazonian spider monkey 11. Six-banded armadillo 12. Scarlet macaw 13. Spectacled bear 14. Viscacha

7 Found all over South America, this animal is named after the bright patches on its face and legs.

It can grow to 20 in (50 cm) in length.

8 Hot sun is not a problem for this animal. Its skin produces a waxy substance that prevents it from getting burned.

Green skin gives camouflage.

9 Hanging around in trees is this animal's favorite activity. It spends most of its life upside down and moves very, very slowly.

10 Highly endangered, this white-bellied primate is only found in the rainforests of Colombia and Venezuela. It uses its long, bushy tail to grip branches.

11 Bony plates cover this animal's back, head, legs, and tail. If threatened, it curls up into a ball for self-defense.

Long, coarse hair covers its "armor."

It has distinctive white markings around the eyes.

12 Noisy shrieks fill the air as these brightly colored birds whizz through the skies above the rainforest. They eat mainly fruit, nuts, and seeds.

13 This animal lives high up in the Andes Mountains, where it forages for food on the ground, as well as up trees.

14 This small, rabbitlike rodent uses its powerful back legs to spring between rocks in the Andes Mountains.

The long, flexible tail helps steer the bird as it speeds through the air.

TEST YOURSELF

STARTER	CHALLENGER	GENIUS!
Red poison dart frog	**Common squirrel monkey**	**Marimonda spider monkey**
Giant leaf frog	**Amazonian palm viper**	**Six-banded armadillo**
Galápagos giant tortoise	**Spectacled bear**	**Viscacha**
Red-footed tortoise	**Pale-throated sloth**	**Capybara**
Green anaconda	**Scarlet macaw**	

Laser beams help focus on distant stars.

② Carved into the walls of a salt mine, this church in Colombia is 656 ft (200 m) under the ground. It is named after the town in which it is located.

③ Perched on top of Mount Corcovado, this colossal statue towers over the city of Rio de Janeiro in Brazil. It is 98 ft (30 m) tall.

① Four telescopes work together as one at this astronomical observatory in Chile. They are built high up in the Atacama Desert, where the air is clear and dry, ensuring better visibility.

The church has 14 chapels, all connected by tunnels.

Human-made wonders

Evidence of the ancient civilizations of South America is found across the continent—from mysterious drawings in the desert to abandoned mountaintop towns. However, there are also many modern superstructures in its big cities. How many of these marvels can you name?

④ In São Paulo, Braz X marks the spot fc this bridge—its two curvin lanes cross over each othe above the Pinheiros Rive

The bridge is suspended from a mast by steel cables.

Each petal is made of aluminum.

Each car travels 7¾ miles (12.5 km) up the mountain.

⑤ The world's highest cable car is also one of the longest rides and takes passengers to Espejo Peak in Venezuela.

⑥ Located in the middle of a square in Buenos Aires, Argentina, this sculpture opens its petals in the morning and closes them at night.

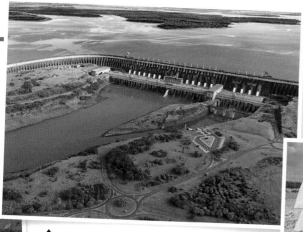

⑧ Rising out of the sand at Brava Beach in Punta del Este, Uruguay, this unusual sculpture is made of cement and iron.

It is also known as *The Hand*.

⑦ Stretching across the Paraná River between Brazil and Paraguay, this huge structure uses flowing water to generate electricity.

The structure is made of adobe, a type of dried mud brick.

⑨ A group of huge designs, around 600 ft (180 m) across on average, were carved into the desert in Peru around 2,000 years ago.

This monkey is one of several animal shapes created here.

⑩ This huge, stepped clay pyramid was built in Peru by the pre-Incan Lima culture around 1,500 years ago.

⑪ High up in the Andes Mountains of Peru, this Inca complex was built around 600 years ago. It is believed to have been a sacred site dedicated to the Sun god.

TEST YOURSELF

STARTER
Machu Picchu
Christ the Redeemer
Mérida Cable Car
Itaipu Dam
Very Large Telescope

CHALLENGER
Floralis Genérica
Salt Cathedral of Zipaquirá
Nazca Lines

GENIUS!
La Mano
Huaca Pucllana
Ponte Octávio Frias de Oliveira

Africa

Africa is a huge landmass, home to the world's biggest sandy desert, as well as rainforests and mountain ranges. With 54 countries—more than any other continent—it is also a land rich in culture, with around 2,000 different languages spoken.

At a glance

Discover some facts and stats about the continent of Africa.

1 Biggest country by area
Algeria stretches from the Mediterranean coast to the desert interior for 919,595 sq miles (2,381,741 sq km).

2 Smallest country by area
The Seychelles is an archipelago of 115 islands off Africa's eastern coast. It has a total area of just 174 sq miles (451 sq km).

3 Biggest city by population
Lagos, Nigeria, has 14.8 million residents in the city, and more than 21 million in the wider metropolitan area.

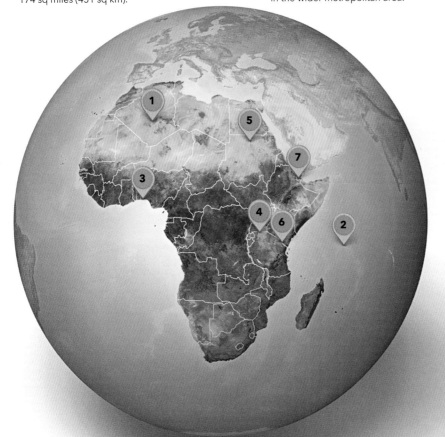

Fantastic festivals

Here are just three festivals celebrated across Africa, from religious ceremonies to masked events.

Timkat
Held every January, this Ethiopian festival celebrates the baptism of Jesus in the River Jordan. It lasts three days and includes a church service, singing, and dancing.

Festima
Music, dancing, and ornate masks are part of this celebration held every two years in Burkina Faso. People from more than 50 villages across six West African nations take part.

International Festival of the Sahara
This festival takes place in the Tunisian desert. There are four days of singing, poetry readings, feasting, camel marathons, and horse races.

4 Biggest lake
Lake Victoria crosses the borders of Uganda, Kenya, and Tanzania. It has an area of 26,560 sq miles (68,880 sq km).

5 Longest river
The Nile runs northward through 11 nations, emptying into the Mediterranean Sea. It is 4,160 miles (6,695 km) long.

6 Highest point
Mount Kilimanjaro in Tanzania is 19,336 ft (5,895 m) high. It is the highest mountain in the world not part of a range.

7 Lowest point
Lake Assal in Djibouti is 512 ft (156 m) below sea level. It is one of the saltiest lakes on Earth.

I don't believe it

Despite it being the second largest continent in the world, Africa has the shortest coastline.

How to help an endangered animal

01. Find a safe enclosure in the Center where the giraffes can live, away from predators and hunters.

02. Start a captive breeding program, which involves the mating of two giraffes in order to produce calves.

03. When ready, reintroduce small groups into the wild. For Rothschild's giraffes, calves are released into the wild after two to three years.

Habitat loss and poaching have endangered the survival of Rothschild's giraffes. In 1979, only 130 remained in the wild. Sanctuaries such as the Giraffe Center in Nairobi, Kenya, have worked hard to increase the number of these giraffes.

04. Monitor the giraffes as they start their lives in the wild, watching out for any potential dangers, such as poachers. It is also important to educate visitors to the Center about giraffes and their habitats.

Luanda

As people move from rural areas looking for jobs, the capital city of Angola has become one of the fastest-growing cities in Africa. With a population of around 7.5 million and rising, Luanda benefits from the country's rich oil reserves, which it trades globally through its busy port.

The Maasai

Living in the Great Rift Valley area of northern Tanzania and southern Kenya, the Maasai people are seminomadic, moving from place to place in search of fresh grazing for their cattle. Numbering around 800,000, they speak a language called Maa, but many also speak the official languages of Tanzania and Kenya; Swahili and English.

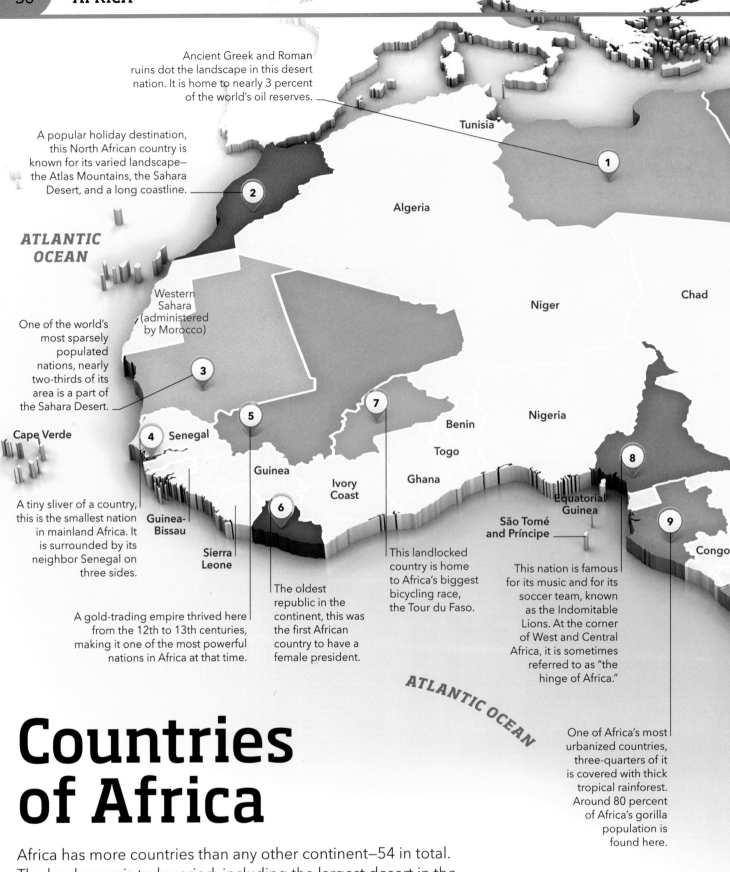

Ancient Greek and Roman ruins dot the landscape in this desert nation. It is home to nearly 3 percent of the world's oil reserves.

A popular holiday destination, this North African country is known for its varied landscape—the Atlas Mountains, the Sahara Desert, and a long coastline.

One of the world's most sparsely populated nations, nearly two-thirds of its area is a part of the Sahara Desert.

A tiny sliver of a country, this is the smallest nation in mainland Africa. It is surrounded by its neighbor Senegal on three sides.

A gold-trading empire thrived here from the 12th to 13th centuries, making it one of the most powerful nations in Africa at that time.

The oldest republic in the continent, this was the first African country to have a female president.

This landlocked country is home to Africa's biggest bicycling race, the Tour du Faso.

This nation is famous for its music and for its soccer team, known as the Indomitable Lions. At the corner of West and Central Africa, it is sometimes referred to as "the hinge of Africa."

One of Africa's most urbanized countries, three-quarters of it is covered with thick tropical rainforest. Around 80 percent of Africa's gorilla population is found here.

ATLANTIC OCEAN

Tunisia

Algeria

Niger

Chad

Western Sahara (administered by Morocco)

Cape Verde

Senegal

Guinea

Nigeria

Benin

Togo

Ghana

Ivory Coast

Guinea-Bissau

Sierra Leone

São Tomé and Príncipe

Equatorial Guinea

Congo

ATLANTIC OCEAN

Countries of Africa

Africa has more countries than any other continent—54 in total. The landscape is truly varied, including the largest desert in the world as well as dense rainforests. Today, its countries are some of the fastest developing in the world.

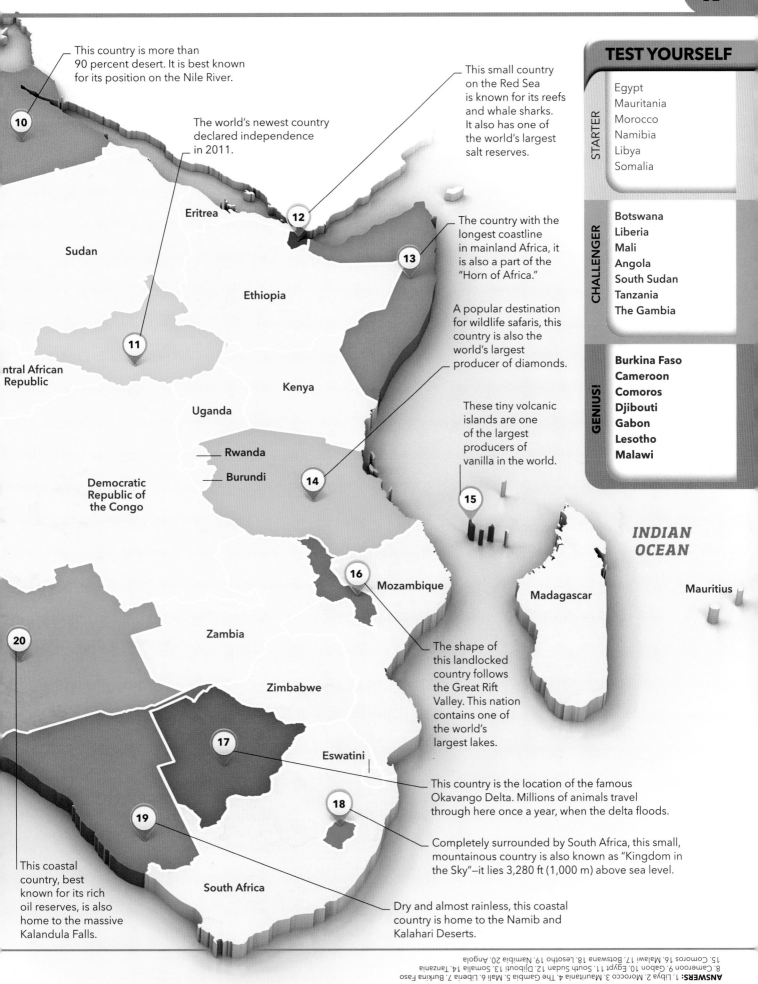

91

This country is more than 90 percent desert. It is best known for its position on the Nile River.

10

The world's newest country declared independence in 2011.

This small country on the Red Sea is known for its reefs and whale sharks. It also has one of the world's largest salt reserves.

Eritrea

12

Sudan

Ethiopia

13

The country with the longest coastline in mainland Africa, it is also a part of the "Horn of Africa."

A popular destination for wildlife safaris, this country is also the world's largest producer of diamonds.

11

ntral African Republic

Kenya

Uganda

These tiny volcanic islands are one of the largest producers of vanilla in the world.

Rwanda

Burundi

Democratic Republic of the Congo

14

15

INDIAN OCEAN

16

Mozambique

Madagascar

Mauritius

The shape of this landlocked country follows the Great Rift Valley. This nation contains one of the world's largest lakes.

20

Zambia

Zimbabwe

17

Eswatini

This country is the location of the famous Okavango Delta. Millions of animals travel through here once a year, when the delta floods.

19

18

Completely surrounded by South Africa, this small, mountainous country is also known as "Kingdom in the Sky"–it lies 3,280 ft (1,000 m) above sea level.

This coastal country, best known for its rich oil reserves, is also home to the massive Kalandula Falls.

South Africa

Dry and almost rainless, this coastal country is home to the Namib and Kalahari Deserts.

TEST YOURSELF

STARTER
Egypt
Mauritania
Morocco
Namibia
Libya
Somalia

CHALLENGER
Botswana
Liberia
Mali
Angola
South Sudan
Tanzania
The Gambia

GENIUS!
Burkina Faso
Cameroon
Comoros
Djibouti
Gabon
Lesotho
Malawi

ANSWERS: 1. Libya 2. Morocco 3. Mauritania 4. The Gambia 5. Mali 6. Liberia 7. Burkina Faso 8. Cameroon 9. Gabon 10. Egypt 11. South Sudan 12. Djibouti 13. Somalia 14. Tanzania 15. Comoros 16. Malawi 17. Botswana 18. Lesotho 19. Namibia 20. Angola

1 Nigeria's capital is located in the heart of the country. It is overlooked by the 2,380-ft (725-m) high Zuma Rock.

2 Egypt's capital city is more than 1,000 years old. It has many historical sites, and the famous pyramids of Giza lie on its outskirts.

This monument is 302 ft (92 m) tall and can be seen from across the capital.

3 Designed in the shape of three palm leaves, the Martyr's Monument in this city commemorates Algeria's independence from France in 1962.

4 Ghana's capital is one of the most modern and wealthy cities in Africa. Parades are held in Black Star Square, also known as the Independence Square.

5 The Senegalese capital has grown from a tiny village into a huge, bustling city and major seaport on the Atlantic coast.

The African Renaissance Monument is 160 ft (49 m) tall and stands just outside the city.

The capital of the DRC is home to Congolese rumba dance music. It is also the city with the largest population in Africa, with just under 15 million inhabitants.

Tunisia

Egypt

Morocco

Libya

Algeria

Niger

Chad

Western Sahara

Mali

Mauritania

Burkina Faso

Benin

Nigeria

Central African Republic

The Gambia

Senegal

Cameroon

Guinea

Ivory Coast

Congo

Guinea-Bissau

Equatorial Guinea

Gabon

Liberia

São Tomé and Príncipe

Sierra Leone

Ghana

Togo

Angola

Capital cities

Africa is home to hundreds of busy, bustling cities, from seaside surfing towns to desert trading centers. Can you name the capital cities picked out on this map across the continent?

7 Ethiopia's capital is home to the headquarters of the African Union, which consists of 54 African country leaders who work toward peace and prosperity.

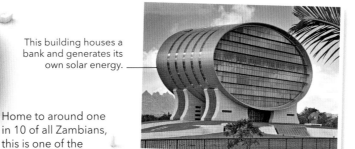

9 With a national park inside its boundaries, Kenya's capital is also home to giraffes, lions, and rhinoceroses. Today, it is one of the major industrial centers in Africa.

The capital of Sudan is positioned where the two branches of the Nile River meet. It was once an ancient Egyptian army camp.

This building houses a bank and generates its own solar energy.

TEST YOURSELF

STARTER
- Addis Ababa
- Algiers
- Cairo
- Cape Town

CHALLENGER
- Accra
- Harare
- Khartoum
- Nairobi
- Port Louis

GENIUS!
- **Abuja**
- **Antananarivo**
- **Dakar**
- **Kinshasa**
- **Lusaka**

Home to around one in 10 of all Zambians, this is one of the fastest-growing cities in all of Africa.

11 The capital of Mauritius is a busy port on the Indian Ocean, known for both its textiles and tourism.

12 This island capital has a large artificial lake—Lake Anosy, in the shape of a heart. It sits high up in the hills of Madagascar.

Djibouti · Eritrea · Sudan · 8 · 7 · Ethiopia · South Sudan · Somalia · Uganda · 9 · Kenya · Rwanda · Burundi · Tanzania · Democratic Republic of the Congo · Malawi · 10 · 14 · Zambia · Zimbabwe · Comoros · 12 · Madagascar · Mauritius · 11 · Mozambique · Eswatini · Botswana · Namibia · South Africa · 13 · Lesotho

You can get to the top of Table Mountain on foot or by cable car.

13 South Africa is the only country in the world with three capital cities. This is one of them. The others are Pretoria and Bloemfontein.

The jacaranda trees bloom here from mid-September to late October.

14 The capital city of Zimbabwe is known as the "Sunshine City" because of its wonderful weather.

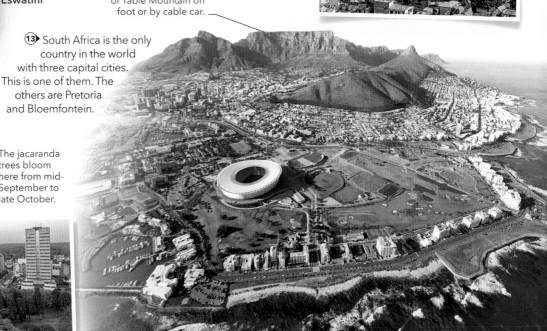

93

The origin of the Eagle of Saladin can be traced back to carvings on ancient temples.

1 This flag belongs to a country that was home to one of the world's oldest civilizations. It symbolizes the nation's independence and rich history.

2 The blue and green on this flag represent this East African country's two peoples—the Issa and the Afar respectively—while the red stands for unity.

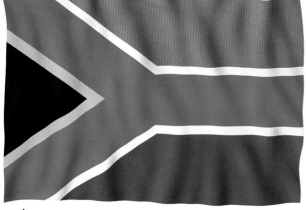

3 The design of this flag conveys unity. It was first used in 1994—the year Nelson Mandela went on to become the country's first black president.

Raise the flag

The symbols and colors on many of the flags of Africa represent what is important to that nation. Some flags show religious symbols, while others emphasize colors that highlight fertile land, Indigenous populations, or political parties. Stars are a common motif, as are animals. Can you match the country to its flag?

4 Home to the Black Star Square, this was the first African country to gain independence, in 1957. The black star on its flag represents freedom.

5 The easternmost country in mainland Africa has the longest coastline. The colors on its flag are based on the United Nations flag.

The Star of Unity represents the five groups of people living in the country.

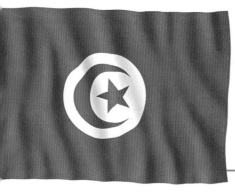

6 This country is close to Europe, and was once part of Turkey. The crescent and star on its flag are a symbol of Islam.

7 This West African country is the richest and most populous in the continent. The green on its flag represents land and the white stands for peace.

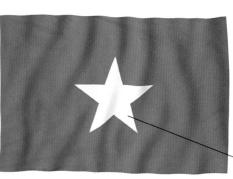

The emblem includes a traditional shield and spears.

⑧ The flag of this landlocked country, located in the center of the continent, features a great crested crane.

⑨ The emblem on the flag of this country, known as Swaziland and renamed by its king in 2018, symbolizes protection from its enemies.

⑩ This flag features the shield and spears of the Maasai people of this East African country, which is known for its wildlife.

⑫ The red diagonal on the flag of this Central African country, which is also the continent's second largest, represents the wars for its independence. The yellow stripes symbolize hope.

The hoe represents agriculture, while the rifle symbolizes this country's fight for independence.

⑪ This country in southeast Africa is famous for its beaches. Green represents the fertile land, black refers to the African continent, and yellow stands for the country's minerals.

⑬ Red proclaims that this north African country's royal family are descended from the Islamic prophet Mohammed. The green five-pointed star was added in 1915.

⑭ The machete on the flag of this country on the western coast of Africa stands for its farmers, while the half-cogwheel highlights industry.

⑮ The smallest country in Africa, the flag for this island nation uses the colors of its political parties to be represented in a striking design.

TEST YOURSELF

STARTER	CHALLENGER	GENIUS!
Kenya	**Morocco**	**Seychelles**
Egypt	**Tunisia**	**Uganda**
South Africa	**Democratic**	**Somalia**
Nigeria	**Republic of Congo**	**Eswatini**
Ghana	**Mozambique**	**Djibouti**
	Angola	

① This tableland area rising out of the Sahara Desert in Mauritania is known for its deep gorges; stony desert areas; and huge, shifting sand dunes.

② Fierce desert winds have sculpted these sandstone plateaus in the Algerian Sahara into jagged peaks and spires that resemble ancient ruins.

This green haven is surrounded by the Western Desert of Egypt. It is known for its freshwater springs, olives, and date palm trees.

The rocky cliffs are about 790 ft (240 m) high.

④ Found in the Ennedi region of Chad, this famous natural arch is 403 ft (123 m) high. It was formed by wind, sand, and rain wearing away at the rock.

ATLANTIC OCEAN

This active volcano last erupted in 2015.

The peak stands 1,213 ft (370 m) tall.

⑥ Towering above the rainforest, this rocky peak, also known as "Great Dog Peak," was once the liquid magma in the core of a volcano. It is now a popular site for rock climbing.

Mediterranean Sea

ATLANTIC OCEAN

⑦ This torrent of white water in the Central African Republic is formed as the M'bari River shoots over the rock cliffs.

⑤ At 9,281 ft (2,829 m) tall, this is the highest peak on the island of Cape Verde. The mountain's black soil has nutrients perfect for growing coffee and fruit trees.

Natural wonders

A huge range of astonishing natural features dot the landscape of Africa, including rocky cliffs that rise out of the vast Sahara Desert in the north, spectacular waterfalls in the lush rainforests of Central Africa, and the dramatic Rift Valley in East Africa.

⑧ Dozens of waterways criss-cross this swampy wetland in Botswana. It supports the world's largest population of elephants.

9 This waterfall in Ethiopia takes its name from the river that pours over it. The clouds of spray created as the waters plunge 150 ft (45 m) give it the nickname the "Great Smoke."

The brown water is rich in silt.

10 This region in East Africa covers an area of 2,500 miles (4,000 km). It is a huge crack in the landscape that was formed by two sections of Earth's crust pulling apart.

11 At 19,340 ft (5,895 m), Africa's highest mountain is this dormant volcano in Tanzania. It is built from the overlapping cones of three volcanoes, with the snow-capped central cone being the highest.

This mountain is permanently snow-capped despite lying near the equator.

12 A massive lake of bubbling lava lies at the top of this active volcano in the Democratic Republic of the Congo. It is one of the most active lava lakes in the world.

INDIAN OCEAN

The ocean shelf has a 492-ft (150-m) drop.

Located on the last bend of the Orange River in South Africa, this desert wilderness is home to various animals, including antelopes, monkeys, and baboons.

13 A popular tourist attraction in Mauritius, constantly flowing sand and mud pour off the ocean shelf, creating the illusion of a waterfall.

These falls lie at the border of two countries.

15 The thundering waters of the Zambezi River, on the border between Zambia and Zimbabwe, drop 354 ft (108 m) here, creating the largest sheet of falling water in the world.

TEST YOURSELF

STARTER	CHALLENGER	GENIUS!
Aloba Arch	**Adrar Plateau**	**Mount Nyiragongo**
Mount Kilimanjaro	**Blue Nile Falls**	**Pico do Fogo**
Okavango Delta	**Hoggar Mountains**	**Pico Cão Grande**
Siwa Oasis	**Great Rift Valley**	**Richtersveld National Park**
Underwater Waterfall	**Boali Falls**	
Victoria Falls		

Rivers and lakes

Africa is criss-crossed with rivers and dotted with lakes. Some African lakes are hot, salty, and inhospitable to life, while others are filled with thousands of species of fish.

The river flows through the city of Cairo in Egypt.

① The longest river in the world flows through several countries in northeast Africa and across the Sahara Desert. It is more than 4,130 miles (6,650 km) long.

Named after the country in which it is located, this freshwater lake in the middle of the desert has been shrinking due to overuse by farming and climate change.

The city of Timbuktu lies on the banks of this river.

③ Curving in a crescent-shaped path from the Guinea Highlands to the Gulf of Guinea in West Africa, this river flows through more than 10 countries.

ATLANTIC OCEAN

Salt is regularly harvested from this lake.

④ Also known as "Lac Rose," this salt lake in Senegal is famous for its bright pink color, which is caused by a type of algae that is attracted to its high salt content.

⑤ This is the only major river to cross the equator twice. It runs through a tropical rainforest and has many stretches of rapids along its course.

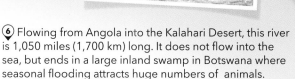

⑥ Flowing from Angola into the Kalahari Desert, this river is 1,050 miles (1,700 km) long. It does not flow into the sea, but ends in a large inland swamp in Botswana where seasonal flooding attracts huge numbers of animals.

TEST YOURSELF

STARTER	CHALLENGER	GENIUS!
Congo River	Lake Assal	Lake Kivu
Lake Chad	Lake Nakuru	Lake Malawi
Lake Victoria	Lake Natron	Lake Tanganyika
Niger River	Lake Retba	Okavango River
Nile River	Limpopo River	Zambezi River

7 Hundreds of bird species flock to this shallow freshwater lake in Kenya, where they eat tiny algae in the water.

The lake is known for its populations of flamingos.

8 Commercial fishing boats are a common sight on this lake, which is Africa's largest and crosses into three countries—Kenya, Tanzania, and Uganda.

9 This lake is about 360 miles (580 km) long and is popular for snorkeling and kayaking. It has up to 3,000 species of freshwater fish, more than any other lake on Earth.

10 Nicknamed the "Killer Lake," this lake has dangerously high levels of carbon dioxide and methane in its deeper layers. It lies on the border of the Democratic Republic of the Congo and Rwanda.

At 410 miles (660 km), the longest freshwater lake in the world crosses four countries.

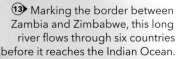

12 This highly saline lake in Djibouti marks the lowest point in Africa. It is surrounded by the Danakil Desert.

A crust of white salt edges the lake.

13 Marking the border between Zambia and Zimbabwe, this long river flows through six countries before it reaches the Indian Ocean.

INDIAN OCEAN

The Kariba Dam, one of the biggest in the world, is built on this river.

The Debengeni Falls drop from the height of 262 ft (80 m).

The bright red color is caused by tiny microorganisms.

15 Fed by hot springs, the water of this salty lake reaches scalding temperatures of 104°F (40°C). Minerals from the springs, volcanic rocks, and ash from a nearby volcano form a pattern on the lake's surface.

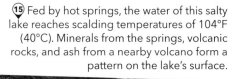

14 This river originates in South Africa and is 1,087 miles (1,750 km) long. Its name means "river of many waterfalls."

ANSWERS: 1. Nile River 2. Lake Chad 3. Niger River 4. Lake Retba 5. Congo River 6. Okavango River 7. Lake Nakuru 8. Lake Victoria 9. Lake Malawi 10. Lake Kivu 11. Lake Tanganyika 12. Lake Assal 13. Zambezi River 14. Limpopo River 15. Lake Natron

① This big cat is comfortable in trees. It will often drag its kill into trees so other predators, such as hyenas, cannot steal it.

The trunks can reach a diameter of 30 ft (9 m).

② Known as the "tree of life," this tree has a barrel-like trunk that allows it to store water in the dry season. It can live for up to 5,000 years.

The small leaves help the tree conserve water.

Its spotted yellow fur gives good camouflage in tall grasses.

The grass turns pink as it dries.

③ This grass grows throughout the savanna. It is tough, and only a few animals, such as wildebeests, are able to eat it.

④ This thorny tree is a feature of the Serengeti. It is one of the few trees that grows in the region and provides food and shade to animals.

Small rock islands, known as kopjes, are found across this region.

TEST YOURSELF

STARTER
Black rhinoceros
Cheetah
Hippopotamus
Leopard
Red oat grass

CHALLENGER
Acacia
Baobab
Secretary bird
Wildebeest

GENIUS!
Fischer's lovebird
Candelabra tree
Usambiro barbet

The Serengeti

Spanning northern Tanzania, the Serengeti grasslands are a vast open area of savanna—rolling plains, broken by the occasional tree. The land here supports a wide range of animal life, from large herbivores that graze on the grasses and trees to the predators that prey on them.

⑤ This big cat has a light build and is the fastest animal on land. It chases its prey at speed, reaching 70 mph (115 km/h) in just three seconds.

⑥ Each year, around 1.5 million of these animals visit the Serengeti as they pass through on their annual migration.

ANSWERS: 1. Leopard 2. Baobab 3. Red oat grass 4. Acacia 5. Cheetah 6. Wildebeest 7. Black rhinoceros 8. Secretary bird 9. Fischer's lovebird 10. Candelabra tree 11. Usambiro barbet 12. Hippopotamus

7 Once plentiful in the Serengeti, this horned herbivore is now critically endangered due to illegal hunting.

Its pointed upper lip helps it pluck leaves and fruit.

8 This long-legged bird of prey gets its name from the quill-like black feathers on its head. It kills its prey, such as snakes, by stomping on it.

Tough scales protect the legs from snakebites.

9 Small but loud, this little parrot is named after a German explorer. It likes to live in pairs.

10 This tree gets its name from its unusual shape. Its branches resemble a very grand candlestick.

Sharp canine teeth can reach 20 in (50 cm) in length.

12 This mammal is very aggressive, making it one of the most dangerous animals in the region. It can weigh up to 6,060 lb (2,750 kg)—twice that of a compact car.

11 This little bird is found only in the Serengeti and Kenya's Maasai Mara National Reserve.

Zebras are also a part of this animal's annual migration.

Biomes

There are eight land biomes in Africa. Across this vast continent, tropical rainforests form a band around the center, mountain ranges spread around its edges, and deserts dominate the north. On the island country of Madagascar, there are several distinct biomes.

Biomes of Africa

Rif Mountains
This grassy range rises up from the Mediterranean coast. Some mountains—including the highest, Mount Tidirhine, at 8,059 ft (2,456 m)—are snowcapped in winter.

Al Hoceima National Park
Rugged cliffs are in this Moroccan coastal park covered in Mediterranean woodland. In the water, Mediterranean monk seals hide in sea caves.

Sahara Desert
This desert covers an area of 3.6 million sq miles (9.2 million sq km), including 10 countries. The Hoggar Mountains in Algeria lie in the center and tower over the desert terrain around them.

Okavango Delta
Once a year, the Okavango River in Botswana floods, resulting in a swampy inland delta dotted with islands and waterways. More than 400 bird species live here.

Amathole Mountains
Thick forests cover this South African mountain range, known for its steep ravines and waterfalls. Above the treeline are grassy meadows, full of flowers.

I don't believe it!
The savanna is home to Earth's tallest animal on land, the giraffe, as well as its biggest land animal, the African elephant.

Animal life

Animals have bodies and skills that enable them to survive in their environments. These African creatures are adapted to living in different habitats, from sweltering deserts to lush forests and dry savannas.

Deathstalker scorpion
To conserve energy in the heat, this desert scorpion with a sharp sting can slow down its body processes. It hunts at night, feeding on insects.

Ring-tailed lemur
This animal keeps its tail in the air to communicate with others when traveling in a group. Strong hands and legs allow it to jump between trees.

Zebra
Some experts believe that the zebra's stripes confuse blood-sucking horseflies, preventing them from landing on this grass-chomping mammal.

Types of biomes

- ▮ Tropical moist broadleaf forest
- ▮ Temperate coniferous forest
- ▮ Desert and dry shrubland
- ▮ Mediterranean forest and woodland
- ▮ Tropical dry broadleaf forest
- ▮ Tropical grassland and savanna
- ▮ Flooded grassland and savanna
- ▮ Mountain grassland

Zakouma National Park
The Salamat River winds its way through the tropical grasslands of this massive park in Chad. Acacia trees and many animals, including elephants, thrive here.

Masoala National Park
This park contains vast swathes of lush tropical forests in Madagascar and is home to half of all flora and fauna in the country, including 19 species of lemur.

Ankarafantsika National Park
With dry forests dotted with lakes, this is a vital conservation area in Madagascar. Endangered animals, from lemurs to birds, live here.

Red Sea reefs

The Red Sea lies off Africa's northeast coast. Extending 174,000 sq miles (450,000 sq km), it is one of the warmest seas in the world. It is also home to coral reefs that support a huge range of creatures, including these beautiful hooded butterflyfish.

Conservation facts

- 🍃 In 2021, conservation efforts have brought the total number of mountain gorillas in the wild–in Uganda, the Congo, and Rwanda–to more than 1,000.

- 🍃 Killed for meat and ivory, the number of forest elephants in West Africa has declined by 86 percent in the past three decades. Local rangers are leading the fight against poachers.

① This animal is the biggest predator on the African savanna. It lives in a big group known as a pride.

Males have a thick, shaggy mane.

② This great ape is humans' closest animal relative. It lives in forests and eats fruit, insects, small animals, and leaves.

Babies are carried by the mother for 3-4 years.

③ Also called the spiderman lizard because of its coloration, this reptile spends its days on rocks in grasslands and deserts.

Males have a long, bright blue tail.

④ Too heavy to fly, the world's largest bird makes a run for it instead. It can reach a speed of 43 mph (70 km/h).

The large ears radiate heat, which keeps the animal from overheating under the hot African Sun.

Long, muscled legs deliver a powerful kick.

⑤ Africa's smallest wild cat hunts shrews, birds, and small reptiles. It is about the same size as a pet cat.

Dark fur under the paws protects its feet from the hot, dry ground.

Amazing animals

⑥ This jumbo-sized animal is the world's largest land mammal. It uses its flexible trunk to spray water, breathe, and collect food.

Famous for its wildlife, Africa is home to many native species, some of which are endangered. The continent's diverse habitats support one-fifth of all known mammal and bird species in the world. Can you identify them all?

ANSWERS: 1. African lion 2. Eastern chimpanzee 3. Mwanza rock agama 4. Common ostrich 5. Black-footed cat 6. African elephant 7. African moon moth 8. Springbok 9. Madagascan sunset moth 10. Okapi 11. Nile monitor lizard 12. Eastern gorilla 13. Meerkat 14. Rothschild's giraffe 15. Lesser flamingo

Males have longer horns than females.

(7) A wide green body gives this insect perfect camouflage against leaves. It sleeps during the day and comes out at night.

(8) South Africa's national animal, this agile antelope springs high into the air in a behavior called "pronking."

White stripes break up the animal's outline in partially sunlit areas.

(9) The markings on this insect's wings change color as it flaps. It is only found on one African island.

(10) This shy rainforest animal is a relative of the giraffe. It uses its long tongue to strip leaves from branches.

(11) Almost 7.2 ft (2.2 m) long, Africa's longest lizard lives near water. It uses its sharp claws and muscular legs to catch its prey.

Long, forked tongue helps detect prey.

Males beat the chest with their hands when threatened.

(12) Strong and heavily built, this animal is the largest of the apes. Males can grow up to 6 ft (1.8 m) tall.

They stand up on their back legs to look for predators.

(13) Teamwork is essential for these alert little animals from the mongoose family. A group of them is called a mob.

(14) The world's tallest mammal grows up to 19¾ ft (6 m) in height. Its long neck allows it to eat the leaves other savanna animals cannot reach.

(15) This bird bends its long neck and uses its beak to filter out tiny food particles from the water. The pigments in the algae it eats turns its feathers pink.

Human-made wonders

Some of the world's most powerful ancient empires have left behind iconic structures in Africa, but this continent is also home to innovative modern buildings designed in concrete and steel. How many of these stunning sites can you identify?

The outer wall of the Great Enclosure is 16 ft (5 m) thick.

① Built around 1,000 years ago, this was the capital city of a powerful kingdom. The Great Enclosure, its largest structure, was built using 900,000 blocks of granite.

② Sand from the Sahara Desert covered and preserved the ruins of this Roman city for nearly a thousand years. Located in the Aurès Mountains, it is often called the "Algerian Pompeii."

Roads are straight and arranged in a grid.

③ More than 200 of these steep-sided structures are found at this site in modern-day Sudan. They were the royal tombs of the Kingdom of Kush.

The roof is made of a thin concrete shell.

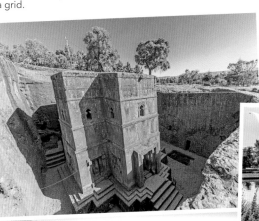

④ This monument celebrates the coming together of the French and British colonies to form the independent nation of Cameroon.

The main structure is 23 ft (7 m) tall.

⑤ Stonemasons carved this Christian church in Ethiopia out of a single rock in the ground. Paths through the surrounding rock link it to 10 similar structures nearby.

⑥ The wavy design of this church in South Africa imitates the shape of the mountain ranges that surround it.

TEST YOURSELF

STARTER	CHALLENGER	GENIUS!
The Great Pyramid and the Sphinx	Great Mosque of Djenné	Bosjes Chapel
Meroë Pyramids	Zeitz MOCAA	Church of St. George, Lalibela
Amphitheatre of El Jem	Reunification Monument	Chefchaouen
Great Zimbabwe	Stone Circles of Senegambia	Timgad

⑦ Located between the Gambia and Senegal Rivers, four groups of rock monuments and burial mounds make up this ancient site that dates from the 3rd century BCE to the 16th century.

⑨ Once used to store maize from across South Africa, this building was redesigned as a modern art gallery. It holds the world's largest collection of modern African art.

Nearly 1,000 stones like this one are spread across 62 miles (100 km).

⑧ Inspired by the Colosseum in Rome, this structure in Tunisia is one of the best-preserved Roman ruins in the world. It was built as a venue for gladiator fights and sporting events.

The stands held up to 35,000 people.

⑩ Many of the walls in this Moroccan town are painted bright blue—it is known as the "Blue Pearl."

116 giant concrete tubes were modified to create spaces for art galleries.

⑪ Built around 700 years ago, this sacred structure in Mali is the largest mud brick building in the world. Fresh mud is added to it every year.

The top of this structure was originally capped with polished limestone.

This massive statue, carved from a single rock, is 66 ft (20 m) tall.

⑫ Ancient Egyptians built this colossal tomb for Pharaoh Khufu along the banks of the Nile River at Giza. It is guarded by a mythical beast with the head of a man and the body of a lion.

EUROPE

Europe

Bounded by the Atlantic and Arctic Oceans to the west and north, Europe is part of the Eurasian landmass. In the southern half of the continent, the Mediterranean Sea lies to the west and the Black Sea to the east.

At a glance

Discover some facts and stats about the continent of Europe.

(1) Biggest country by area
Russia (European section), at 1,527,350 sq miles (3,955,818 sq km), is 28 times larger than Europe's second largest, Ukraine.

(2) Smallest country by area
Vatican City, with an area of 0.17 sq miles (0.44 sq km), is the size of 61 soccer fields. It is found in the Italian city of Rome.

(3) Biggest city by population
Moscow, Russia, has 13.2 million residents in the city, and more than 20 million in the wider metropolitan area.

(4) Biggest lake
Lake Lodoga in Russia is the largest of Europe's 500,000 lakes. It has an area of 6,785 sq miles (17,670 sq km).

(5) Longest river
The Volga runs 2,193 miles (3,530 km) through Russia's biggest cities before emptying into the Caspian Sea.

(6) Highest point
Mount Elbrus, a dormant volcano, stands at 18,510 ft (5,642 m) high. It is the highest peak in the Caucasus Mountains.

(7) Lowest point
The seabed of the Caspian Sea—the world's largest inland body of water—lies 92 ft (28 m) below sea level.

In numbers

Population
750 million

Size
3,930,000 sq miles (10,180,000 sq km)

Countries
46

I don't believe it

Vinárna Čertovka Street in Prague, Czech Republic, is just 20 in (50 cm) wide, yet has its own traffic lights.

How to stay warm in Iceland

The Blue Lagoon is one of Iceland's most visited attractions. Its milky-blue water is rich in minerals and has an average temperature of 102°F (39°C) all year round.

01. The Svartsengi geothermal power plant pumps water over hot rocks underground and uses the steam generated to drive turbines to make electricity—but it's also a spa!

02. The water is cooled, then flows into the lagoon, but it's still very hot. The blue color comes from algae, which are able to survive the heat.

The Sámi

Europe is ethnically diverse, with more than 200 languages spoken. One of the few nomadic peoples left in the continent are the Sámi people. This Indigenous population follows reindeer herds as they move across northern Scandinavia and Russia, living in traditional temporary homes, known as lavvo tents. At parties and festivals, the Sámi wear their distinctive traditional clothing called gátki.

Fantastic festivals

Thousands of festivals, some centuries old, dot the calendar of this colorful continent each year.

St. Patrick's Day
Every March 17th, Ireland goes green, plays music, and parties to celebrate the life of a 5th-century Christian missionary.

Amsterdam Tulip Festival
The Netherlands' largest city springs into life from late March to early May with thousands of colorful tulips in bloom.

Zagreb International Folklore Festival
Held since 1966, and typically in July, this is Croatia's largest celebration of traditional culture, fashion, arts, and dance.

03. The water is not just hot, it's rich in minerals from the rocks. The Blue Lagoon is a popular spa, so take a dip—more than 1 million people do every year!

Ice hotel

Since 1990, a hotel carved out of solid blocks of river ice has welcomed visitors to Jukkasjärvi in northern Sweden. Every spring, it melts into the River Torne before being rebuilt again in the winter months.

Countries of Europe

The borders within Europe have been drawn and redrawn many times in more than 3,000 years of history. Today, the continent is made up of 46 countries, ranging from large farming or industrial nations to tiny microstates.

TEST YOURSELF

STARTER
France
Germany
Iceland
Ireland
Poland
Spain

CHALLENGER
Belgium
Estonia
Liechtenstein
Monaco
Norway

GENIUS!
Albania
Bulgaria
Moldova
Slovakia
Croatia
Ukraine

This mountainous country has a spectacular coastline of deep sea inlets–known as fjords. The island group of Svalbard is also a part of this country.

Norwegian Sea

This is Europe's largest economy. It was divided in two after World War II– East and West–and reunited in 1989.

This island nation is located just south of the Arctic Circle. It has about 200 volcanoes, out of which 30 are active, and is known for its black volcanic soil.

ATLANTIC OCEAN

This lush, green island is made up of two countries, and the one to the north is part of the UK.

This country is known as one of the Low Countries, along with the Netherlands, because of its flat land. It houses the European Union headquarters.

Say *bonjour* to baguettes, croissants, and the world's most famous bicycle race that is held annually in this nation.

This tiny mountain nation has a population of 40,000; is ruled by a prince; and is the world's biggest manufacturer of false teeth.

This popular holiday destination's territory includes the Balearic Islands in the Mediterranean Sea and the Canary Islands in the Atlantic Ocean.

Europe's second smallest state, after Vatican City, has just 3.8 miles (6 km) of land borders. More than 30 percent of its citizens are millionaires.

Sweden

Denmark

North Sea

Netherlands

United Kingdom

Luxembourg

Switzerland

Andorra

Portugal

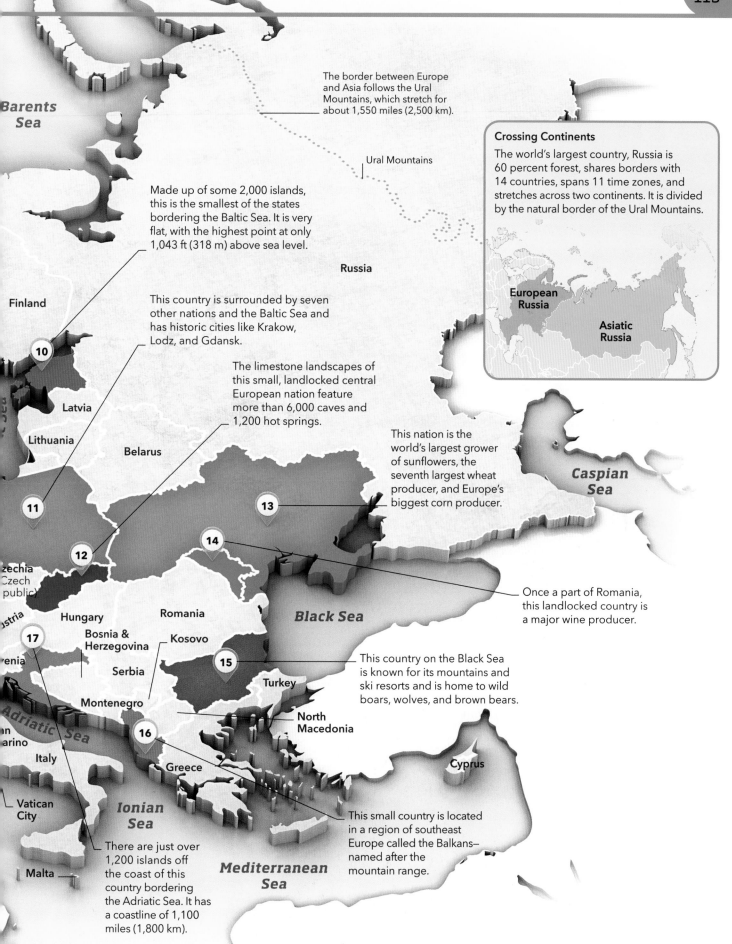

Barents
Sea

The border between Europe
and Asia follows the Ural
Mountains, which stretch for
about 1,550 miles (2,500 km).

Ural Mountains

Crossing Continents

The world's largest country, Russia is
60 percent forest, shares borders with
14 countries, spans 11 time zones, and
stretches across two continents. It is divided
by the natural border of the Ural Mountains.

**European
Russia**

**Asiatic
Russia**

Russia

Made up of some 2,000 islands,
this is the smallest of the states
bordering the Baltic Sea. It is very
flat, with the highest point at only
1,043 ft (318 m) above sea level.

Finland

This country is surrounded by seven
other nations and the Baltic Sea and
has historic cities like Krakow,
Lodz, and Gdansk.

10

Latvia

The limestone landscapes of
this small, landlocked central
European nation feature
more than 6,000 caves and
1,200 hot springs.

Lithuania

Belarus

This nation is the
world's largest grower
of sunflowers, the
seventh largest wheat
producer, and Europe's
biggest corn producer.

**Caspian
Sea**

11

13

zechia
Czech
public)

12

14

Once a part of Romania,
this landlocked country is
a major wine producer.

ustria

Hungary

Romania

Black Sea

Bosnia &
Herzegovina

Kosovo

enia

17

Serbia

15

This country on the Black Sea
is known for its mountains and
ski resorts and is home to wild
boars, wolves, and brown bears.

Turkey

Adriatic Sea

Montenegro

16

North
Macedonia

an
arino

Italy

Cyprus

Vatican
City

Greece

**Ionian
Sea**

This small country is located
in a region of southeast
Europe called the Balkans—
named after the
mountain range.

There are just over
1,200 islands off
the coast of this
country bordering
the Adriatic Sea. It has
a coastline of 1,100
miles (1,800 km).

Malta

**Mediterranean
Sea**

Capital cities

Although one of the smaller continents, Europe boasts a diverse range of famous capitals. Incredible architecture—from grand palaces and parliaments to colorful old towns—tells the long history of many of these cities. Today, they are also popular tourist destinations and seats of political power.

① The world's northernmost capital lies at the foothills of Mount Esja. The city runs mainly on geothermal power harnessed from Iceland's underground hot springs.

② This maritime city in Denmark is known for its colorful houses, some of which date back to the 1600s.

The city's most famous canal is 1,480 ft (450 m) long.

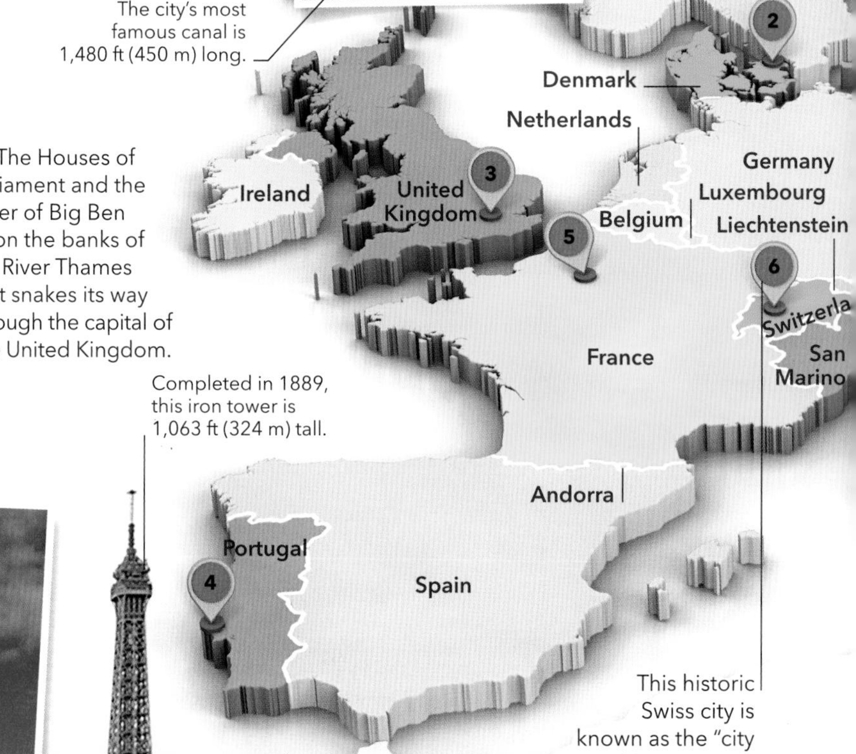

1
Iceland
Finland
Sweden
Norway
2
Denmark
Netherlands
Germany
Luxembourg
Liechtenstein
Ireland
United Kingdom
3
Belgium
5
6
Switzerla
San Marino
France
Andorra
Portugal
4
Spain

③ The Houses of Parliament and the tower of Big Ben lie on the banks of the River Thames as it snakes its way through the capital of the United Kingdom.

The Discoveries Monument features 33 of the country's most well-known explorers.

④ The capital of Portugal sits where the Tagus River meets the sea. The Discoveries Monument, honoring the country's maritime explorers, looks out across the waters.

Completed in 1889, this iron tower is 1,063 ft (324 m) tall.

⑤ Located on the River Seine, this city is home to the iconic Eiffel Tower. It is also called the "City of Light," as it was among the first European cities to use gas street lamps.

This historic Swiss city is known as the "city of fountains." A 13th-century clock tower with mechanical puppets is an iconic landmark here.

7 Named after the river on which it is situated, this Russian city is the largest capital city in Europe. It is home to St. Basil's Cathedral, which is famous for its colorful domes.

8 A major tourist destination, this Latvian city is known for its striking architecture and bustling markets. It has a medieval Old Town at its center.

9 One of the most important landmarks of Ukraine, the Motherland statue is located in this city.

This statue weighs about 550 tons and took two years to build.

Estonia

Russia

Latvia

Lithuania

Belarus

Poland

Czechia (Czech Republic)

Ukraine

Slovakia

Moldova

Austria

Hungary

Romania

Slovenia

Serbia

Montenegro

Bulgaria

Croatia

Bosnia and Herzegovina

Kosovo

North Macedonia

Turkey

Italy

Greece

Vatican City

Albania

Malta

Cyprus

Formed by three cities coming together, the capital of Hungary had the first underground train line in mainland Europe.

The church is 354 ft (108 m) tall.

11 This Croatian city is a mix of its medieval past and modern museums and cafes. The main cathedral has two towers that can be seen from nearly all parts of the capital.

12 Horse-drawn carriages are a common sight across this Austrian city. It is also home to one of the largest palace complexes in the world—the Hofburg.

13 Europe's oldest capital city is in Greece. High on a rocky hill, the ancient citadel of the Acropolis looks over the modern streets below.

Nearly two-thirds of the Colosseum was destroyed by a series of earthquakes.

14 The capital of Italy was the biggest city in the world 2,000 years ago. Perhaps its best-known landmark is the Colosseum, the largest amphitheater in the Roman Empire.

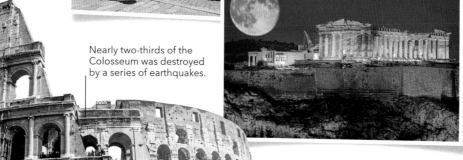

TEST YOURSELF

STARTER
- London
- Copenhagen
- Rome
- Paris
- Moscow

CHALLENGER
- **Reykjavik**
- **Lisbon**
- **Vienna**
- **Bern**
- **Athens**

GENIUS!
- **Riga**
- **Zagreb**
- **Kyiv**
- **Budapest**

ANSWERS: 1. Reykjavik 2. Copenhagen 3. London 4. Lisbon 5. Paris 6. Bern 7. Moscow 8. Riga 9. Kyiv 10. Budapest 11. Zagreb 12. Vienna 13. Athens 14. Rome

Raise the flag

Some of the oldest national flags in the world, as well as some of the newest, are flown by European countries. The break-up of the Soviet Union—a giant country made up of Russia and some neighboring nations—resulted in many new countries across Europe and Asia, each with their own distinctive and symbolic flag.

1 With a radiant Sun at its centre, this flag belongs to a country bordered by five others – Greece, Bulgaria, Albania, Serbia, and Kosovo.

2 The flag of the largest country in the world was originally used by its navy. After a revolution in 1917, a different flag was used until 1991, when this flag was adopted again.

3 This is the flag of an ancient nation of mountains and many islands, which shares its longest land border with Bulgaria.

4 Famous for its Christmas markets, this nation is the birthplace of scientist Albert Einstein and composer Ludwig van Beethoven.

The emblem includes the papal crown.

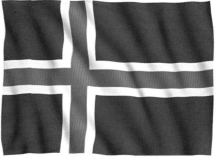

5 White represents the ice from glaciers, while red represents the fire produced by this island nation's many active volcanoes.

6 This square flag, featuring the crossed keys of St. Peter, flies over a state so small that it is enclosed entirely within another country's capital city.

7 This is the flag of a country in the south of Europe, known for its colorful festivals.

The white diagonal cross of St. Andrew of Scotland.

8 Three crosses—two red and one white—represent three of the four countries that make up this nation.

9 The largest country to fly a square flag lies in the Alps and is known for its chocolate and cuckoo clocks.

10 Red symbolizes courage, strength, and bloodshed on the flag of this nation that is found in the Eastern Mediterranean.

11 The yellow triangle on this flag of one of Europe's newest nations mirrors the shape of the country. Its three points represent the nation's three largest ethnic groups.

TEST YOURSELF

STARTER
- United Kingdom
- France
- Germany
- Spain
- Switzerland

CHALLENGER
- **Norway**
- **Portugal**
- **Russia**
- **Iceland**
- **Greece**

GENIUS!
- **Albania**
- **Andorra**
- **Bosnia and Herzegovina**
- **North Macedonia**
- **Vatican City**

This country is known as the land of the eagle, after the double-headed emblem of its coat of arms.

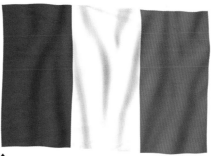

12 Since 1848, this tricolor flag has been flying over this popular tourist destination known for its art, fine food, and wines.

13 Designed in 1821, this flag belongs to a nation that was once ruled by Vikings.

Green represents hope for the future.

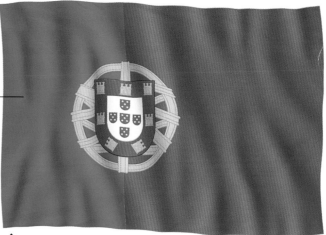

14 This tiny country, known for its ski resorts, lies in the Pyrenees Mountain range between France and Spain.

15 The navigation tool on the coat of arms of this flag represents the history of exploration of the nation bordering Spain.

① Every year, melting water sculpts these hollows and pockets to form new shapes and patterns in the ice. Gleaming blue, they are part of an ice cap that covers almost all of southern Iceland.

The Bridal Veil waterfall is one of three large waterfalls here.

② This coastal inlet was carved out by a glacier. Almost 10 miles (16 km) long, it is lined by steep cliffs.

ATLANTIC OCEAN

③ Wind, rain, and ice carved these jagged formations into the side of a hill in Switzerland during the last ice age. The boulders on top protect the formations from wearing away.

Each conical structure is 33-49 ft (10-15 m) high.

North Sea

The tallest hill of sand in Europe lies in Arcachon Bay, France. It rises to a height of 360 ft (110 m) and is creeping inland.

⑤ More than 40,000 columns make up this extraordinary site in Ireland. It was formed by rapidly cooling lava 60 million years ago, although a legend holds that Celtic hero Fin McCool built it as a pathway to his enemy.

This limestone canyon in Sardinia, Italy, is popularly known as "Europe's Grand Canyon." At its narrowest point, it is only 13 ft (4 m) wide.

The large "skylight" in its roof is 52 ft (16 m) wide.

⑦ Waves from the Atlantic Ocean carved this iconic landmark on the Algarve Coast in Portugal. It can only be reached by boat or by swimming.

Natural wonders

From curious rock formations and deep fjords (sea inlets) to glittering ice caves and twisted trees, Europe is home to many fascinating natural features and spectacular landscapes.

All seven formations were once part of a single mountain.

8 Also known as the Seven Strong Men, these Russian rock pillars in the Ural Mountains were shaped by wind and water. They are 100–138 ft (30–42 m) tall and have flat tops.

9 In the middle of forest and grassland lies this mysterious sandy area, known as the Ukrainian Sahara. However, it is not a desert, but is dotted with grass and shrubs.

10 The highest peak in Europe is 18,510 ft (5,642 m) tall. Located in the Caucasus Mountains in Russia, it is a dormant volcano.

Black Sea

These bizarrely shaped trees are 90–100 years old.

11 Nearly 400 pine trees in these Polish woodlands have a 90-degree bend in their trunks. Scientists have yet to find an explanation for this phenomenon.

Ionian Sea

Mediterranean Sea

The pyramid-shaped peak is almost perfectly symmetrical.

The pool is also known as "eye of the Earth."

12 Found on Dinara Mountain in Croatia, this pool of water is 410 ft (125 m) deep. It is the source of the 62-mile (100-km) long river with which it shares its name.

13 This four-sided peak in the Alps rises to a height of 14,692 ft (4,478 m). It soars above the town of Zermatt in Switzerland on one side and Cervinia in Italy on the other.

TEST YOURSELF

STARTER	CHALLENGER	GENIUS!
Matterhorn	**Manpupuner stone giants**	**Geirangerfjord**
Crooked Forest	**Vatnajökull glacier caves**	**Gola su Gorropu gorge**
Benagil sea cave		**Pyramides d'Euseigne**
Mount Elbrus	**Cetina River Spring**	**Dune du Pilat**
Giant's Causeway	**Oleshky Sands**	

1 Ireland's longest river is 240 miles (380 km) long and flows past Limerick Castle. According to legend, its waters hold a monster called Cata.

At 459 ft (140 m), Jet d'Eau is one of the tallest fountains in the world.

2 Europe's largest alpine lake forms part of the border between France and Switzerland. The Rhône River flows through it.

3 At 215 miles (346 km), this river runs through southern England, to London, and into the North Sea. Through a massive clean-up campaign, this once-dirty river is now home to more than 100 species of fish.

4 Located in Slovenia, this large lake is nestled within the Julian Alps. Its crystal-clear waters are heated by thermal springs to 79°F (26°C).

Tower Bridge was constructed over this river in the late 1800s.

The Church of the Assumption sits on the lake's only island.

Notre-Dame Cathedral is located on Île de la Cité, Paris, an island on this river.

5 This French river flows from Burgundy, through Paris and Le Havre, before emptying into the English Channel.

ATLANTIC OCEAN

North Sea

Bay of Biscay

6 A major transportation link between central and northern Europe, many famous castles and cities, including Basel, Cologne, and Bonn, are located on its banks.

The Vasco da Gama Bridge is the second-longest bridge in Europe.

7 This river flows westward, passing through Spain to Lisbon in Portugal, before reaching the Atlantic Ocean.

Ponte Sant Angelo Bridge, also called the Bridge of Hadrian, crosses this river.

8 According to legend, the city of Rome was founded on the banks of Italy's third-largest river. It meets the sea at Ostia, the port city of ancient Rome.

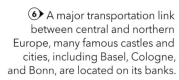

Rivers and lakes

Europe has a large number of rivers and lakes, especially in its northern regions, because of melting glaciers and other geological processes. The continent contains 90 rivers that are more than 186 miles (300 km) long, and hundreds more shorter stretches of flowing water.

9 More than 200 smaller rivers flow into Europe's longest river, which winds 2,193 miles (3,530 km) through Russia to the Caspian Sea.

The Nizhny Novgorod soccer stadium in Russia stands on the riverbank.

This massive Russian lake is the largest in Europe, with a total area of about 6,834 sq miles (17,700 sq km).

This river winds 651 miles (1,047 km) through Poland's biggest cities, including Warsaw, Kraków, and Gdańsk.

Caspian Sea

Black Sea

Mediterranean Sea

This mountain range shares its name with the lake.

12 Europe's second-longest river flows through 10 countries and four capital cities, including Vienna and Budapest (shown below), before emptying into the Black Sea.

The river flows a total of 1,770 miles (2,860 km).

This river flows through a canyon, which is 4,300 ft (1,300 m) deep.

13 Dotted with 69 sets of rapids, this 99-mile (158-km) long river forms part of the border between Montenegro and Bosnia and Herzegovina.

14 Flanked by mountains, Italy's largest lake covers 142 sq miles (367 sq km). St. Francis of Assisi founded a monastery on its largest island in 1220.

TEST YOURSELF

STARTER	CHALLENGER	GENIUS!
Thames River	Volga River	Shannon River
Rhine River	Danube River	Tara River
Seine River	Lake Garda	Lake Ladoga
Tiber River	Tagus River	Vistula River
Lake Geneva	Lake Bled	

① This cheese has been made from goat and sheep milk since the time of the ancient Greeks. Its name is a Greek word for "slice."

② A traditional delicacy of Latvia, this shallow, round pie contains a stuffing made of carrot paste, potato, and caraway seeds.

It is crimped, and is stuffed with meat and vegetables.

The base is traditionally made using rye flour.

③ This Italian cheese is made of cow milk—each wheel uses nearly 145 gallons (550 liters)! It is a hard cheese that is grated onto dishes.

④ This food from Cornwall, England, is traditionally known as an "oggy." It was first baked as portable food for miners in the region.

Flavors of Europe

From potatoes to pizzas, some foods in Europe have protected status to prevent poor imitations from being passed off as the original from a particular geographical area. How many of these fine foods can you name?

⑤ A holiday treat, this German almond paste is named after the city in which it is produced.

This castle, made of the sweet paste, was on display at a famous local sweet shop.

⑥ This nutty-flavored vegetable is grown only on one of the Channel Islands in fewer than two dozen farms.

The light brown skin is very thin and delicate.

⑦ Regarded as one of Portugal's most iconic sweet delicacies, these were first made by nuns more than 400 years ago to sell to passing travelers.

The paper-thin dough is filled with a sweet egg custard.

8 ▶ This finger-thin, dry Polish sausage is usually eaten cold— either with crackers or wrapped in cheese.

The sausages are usually 12 in (30 cm) long.

9 Swedish for "spit cake," this dessert is made from eggs, sugar, and potato flour, cooked on a skewer (spit) over a fire.

The batter is squeezed in circles to create a conical tower.

It is cooked in a wood-fired oven.

10 ▶ This Italian food is made with fresh tomatoes, buffalo milk mozzarella, and basil. The colors match the country's flag, and it is named after the city of origin.

11 ▶ A popular Christmas treat in Spain, this hard, white nougat is made with egg whites, honey, sugar, and toasted nuts.

The nougat is usually made of almonds.

12 A protected food in France since 2018, this dish is fermented for two to nine weeks before serving.

This sour dish is made from fresh, white cabbage.

13 ▶ This famous sparkling wine is packed with bubbles and can only be made in a particular region of France, after which it is named.

The drink can be identified by its color and fizzy bubbles.

The rye dough is usually stuffed with rice pudding or porridge.

14 ▶ This savory Finnish pastry is shaped by hand, and is also popular in Russia and Estonia.

TEST YOURSELF

STARTER
Champagne
Cornish pasty
Feta
Jersey Royal potatoes
Pizza Napoletana

CHALLENGER
Alsatian Sauerkraut
Karelian pie
Parmigiano-Reggiano
Spettkaka

GENIUS!
Kabanos
Lübeck marzipan
Pastel de Tentúgal
Sklandrausis
Turrón de Alicante

Biomes

There are eight land biomes across Europe, each with similar features, including landscape and wildlife. Most of this continent has a temperate climate with cool winters and mild summers, such as the Caledonian Forest, while other regions have a Mediterranean climate, as seen in parts of Spain. Subzero temperatures are common in the Arctic, including the Kola Peninsula.

In numbers

35%
The percentage of Europe's land covered by different types of forests.

26,000
The number of protected areas of land in the continent, which ensures unique habitats are not destroyed.

18,510 ft
(5,642 m) The height of Mount Elbrus, Europe's highest peak.

280
The number of different insect species that live in a single oak tree.

Biomes of Europe

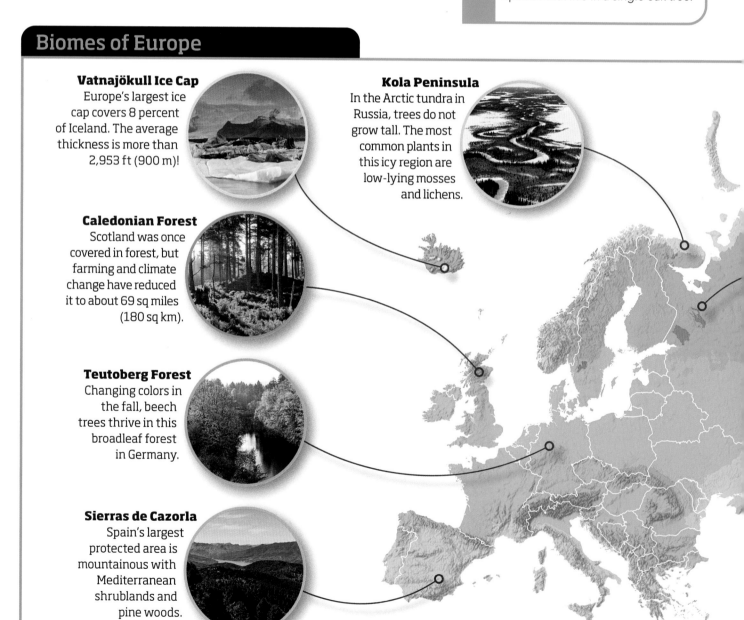

Vatnajökull Ice Cap
Europe's largest ice cap covers 8 percent of Iceland. The average thickness is more than 2,953 ft (900 m)!

Kola Peninsula
In the Arctic tundra in Russia, trees do not grow tall. The most common plants in this icy region are low-lying mosses and lichens.

Caledonian Forest
Scotland was once covered in forest, but farming and climate change have reduced it to about 69 sq miles (180 sq km).

Teutoberg Forest
Changing colors in the fall, beech trees thrive in this broadleaf forest in Germany.

Sierras de Cazorla
Spain's largest protected area is mountainous with Mediterranean shrublands and pine woods.

Conservation facts

🍃 In 2021, a new national park was created in North Macedonia to protect the Shar Mountains (pictured).

🍃 Dams removed from rivers flowing into the Danube Delta in Ukraine are helping provide freshwater and repopulate the area with wildlife.

🍃 For years, red kite birds were endangered in the UK. In 1989, young kites from Sweden were introduced in the UK, and today, there are around 4,600 breeding pairs.

Types of biomes

▦ Temperate broadleaf forest	▦ Temperate coniferous forest
▦ Desert and dry shrubland	▦ Temperate grassland and savanna
▦ Mediterranean forest and woodland	▦ Boreal forest
▦ Tundra	▦ Ice

Vodlozersky National Park
Ileksa River runs through this boreal forest in Russia. Made up of spruce and pine forests that have never been cut down, this biome is also known as taiga.

Kalmykia Desert
Climate change and overgrazing is turning this former grassland in Russia into a sandy, dry desert. Unusual sand pillars dot the barren landscape.

Pontic-Caspian steppe
Stretching over six countries in eastern Europe, mountains break up this area of low plains covered in grassland, herbs, and flowers.

Animal life

From amphibians to mammals, here are three creatures that are found in different habitats across Europe, including forests and woodlands.

Iberian tree frog
With distinct dark stripes along its body, this agile frog lives in Spain, Portugal, and southwestern France. Its toe pads work like suction cups to climb smooth, wet tree leaves.

European bison
Europe's largest wild animal is found in forests throughout Poland, Belarus, and Russia. Its powerful jaws can chew through tough sedges, grasses, and tree bark.

Eurasian treecreeper
Perfectly camouflaged against the bark, this small bird has strong curved claws to grip trees as it hops like a mouse up the trunk. It eats insects using its long, curved bill.

Mediterranean gorgonians

Found in the Mediterranean Sea, gorgonians are a type of coral that create underwater forests and provide habitats for fish and other marine species. They are under threat from fishing boats that trawl the sea bed.

Amazing animals

From wild cats and canines to colorful butterflies and tiny bats, Europe is home to many fascinating creatures. Human activity has reduced the habitats of some larger animals, but the continent's rich and vibrant wildlife continues to thrive.

① This predator is the ancestor of all domestic dogs and is found in eastern and northern Europe. It hunts in groups, or packs, for fish, birds, deer, boar, and smaller mammals.

② Shy of humans, this elusive hunter lives in woodlands across most of Europe. It hunts mice and other small mammals.

Webbed feet help it swim fast.

③ Found in northern Europe, this seabird can hold many fish at once in its large, colorful beak. It is an excellent diver and hunts under water.

It is named after the rounded shape of its ears.

④ Nesting in burrows on sandy banks in southern Europe, this brightly colored bird uses its curved, dagger-shaped bill to catch insects.

⑤ This tiny flying mammal is only 1½ in (4 cm) long and weighs only 0.3 oz (9 g). It is nocturnal, hunting for insects by night and roosting in caves and buildings by day.

Long, pointed tail feathers help it make quick changes in direction midflight.

⑥ Found in the mountains of Romania, this agile, goatlike animal can run as fast as 30 mph (50 km/h) and move nimbly on rocky terrain and steep slopes.

Hooked horns are used for defense against predators.

⑦ Found mostly in Spain, Portugal, and Andorra, this furry creature lives mostly underwater in streams. It has webbed feet for swimming and uses its tail as a rudder.

The long, flattened snout helps it to sniff out prey.

Kids stay with their mother for up to three years.

8 ▶ Named after the large eyespots on its wings that look like the tail feathers of a colorful bird, this insect is found all over Europe.

The eyespots confuse and startle predators.

9 ▶ A member of the weasel family, this animal is found in wooded areas all over Europe. It is Croatia's national animal.

Sharp, partially retractable claws help it climb the tree after which it is named.

Males have a narrow, black bill.

The horns are up to 31½ in (80 cm) long.

Ears have tufted tips.

11 ▶ Found only in southwest Europe, this is the most endangered cat in the world. It lives alone and hunts birds, rabbits, and rodents.

10 ▶ Found near still or slow-flowing water, such as streams, small rivers, and lakes, this bird hunts fish by diving into water and snapping it up.

It has a wingspan of 2–3 in (6–8 cm).

Long white-and-black fur under its chin forms a beard.

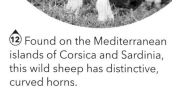

12 ▶ Found on the Mediterranean islands of Corsica and Sardinia, this wild sheep has distinctive, curved horns.

13 ▶ Found throughout Europe, this reptile prefers dry habitats, such as beaches and dunes. It hibernates in self-dug burrows for more than half of the year.

The sides of a male's body turn green during the mating season.

It stands upright and whistles loudly when it senses danger.

14 ▶ This ground-living squirrel stays in its burrow through the winter, and relies on tender shoots for food. It is found in meadows in the Alps.

15 ▶ Despite its name, this insect is relatively common in most parts of Europe. The bright patterns on its wings flash in the sunlight.

The blue underside of its mouth and throat warns predators to stay away.

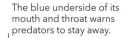

16 ◀ Found mostly in grasslands and forests in southeast Europe, this reptile hatches from the egg pale brown but develops bright skin over time.

TEST YOURSELF

STARTER	CHALLENGER	GENIUS!
European bee-eater	**Pine marten**	**European mouflon**
Atlantic puffin	**Scarce swallowtail butterfly**	**European green lizard**
Eurasian wolf	**Common kingfisher**	**Carpathian chamois**
European wildcat	**Iberian lynx**	**Pyrenean desman**
European peacock butterfly	**Lesser horseshoe bat**	**Sand lizard**
		Alpine marmot

This building dates from the early 13th century.

(1) Built into a cave mouth halfway up a 403-ft (123-m) tall cliff in Slovenia, this is the largest cave fortress in the world.

All of the sculptures represent human emotions.

(2) At 1,104 ft (336 m) high, this is the world's tallest bridge. It crosses the Tarn River in France and took three years to build.

Seven giant concrete piers support the bridge.

(4) The pride of Prague, capital of the Czech Republic, this is one of the world's oldest working timepieces and has displayed the time for more than 600 years.

(3) This public garden in Oslo contains 212 statues in bronze, cast iron, or granite, all made by Norwegian sculptor Gustav Vigeland.

Human-made wonders

Europe is full of extraordinary buildings and superstructures from across the ages, including prehistoric stone circles, leaning towers, brilliant bridges, fairytale castles, and Ferris wheels. How many can you identify?

This clock also displays the relative positions of the Sun, the Moon, and constellations.

The wheel is 443 ft (135 m) tall.

(6) This fairytale fortress was commissioned in 1868 by King Ludwig II of Bavaria. Unlike other castles, it was built only as a lavish retreat and not for protection.

(5) This giant Ferris wheel is located on the south bank of the River Thames and offers incredible views across the UK's capital.

This castle stands atop a rugged hill overlooking a village.

ANSWERS: 1. Predjama Castle 2. Millau Viaduct 3. Vigeland Park 4. Astronomical Clock 5. London Eye 6. Neuschwanstein Castle 7. Stonehenge 8. Leaning Tower of Pisa 9. Monasteries of Meteora 10. La Sagrada Família 11. Cube Houses 12. The Church of Hallgrímur

Most stones weigh between 25 to 30 tons.

It has six open galleries with columns and arches.

7 These standing stones in the UK are one of Europe's most famous prehistoric structures. Experts are still unclear about what they were used for.

The bell towers are made of sandstone.

8 The alarming slant of this Italian bell tower, completed in the late 1300s, has made it a must-see attraction for visitors.

The cliffs are also known as "columns from the sky."

9 Perched on top of steep sandstone pillars, these buildings were once the monasteries for Eastern Orthodox monks in Greece.

Each cube tilts 45 degrees on its side.

10 Work on this ornate church in Barcelona, Spain, began in 1886 and is still ongoing. When finished, it will feature 18 tall spires.

This is Iceland's largest church.

11 These square-shaped houses, designed by Dutch architect Piet Blom, are an abstract representation of trees built above a pedestrian bridge in Rotterdam.

12 This church's design mimics the features of Iceland's landscape, such as basalt columns and glaciers. A gigantic pipe organ weighing 28 tons is kept inside the church.

TEST YOURSELF

STARTER	CHALLENGER	GENIUS!
Leaning Tower of Pisa	La Sagrada Familia	The Church of Hallgrimur
London Eye	Millau Viaduct	Vigeland Park
Neuschwanstein Castle	Predjama Castle	Cube Houses
Stonehenge	Monasteries of Meteora	Astronomical Clock

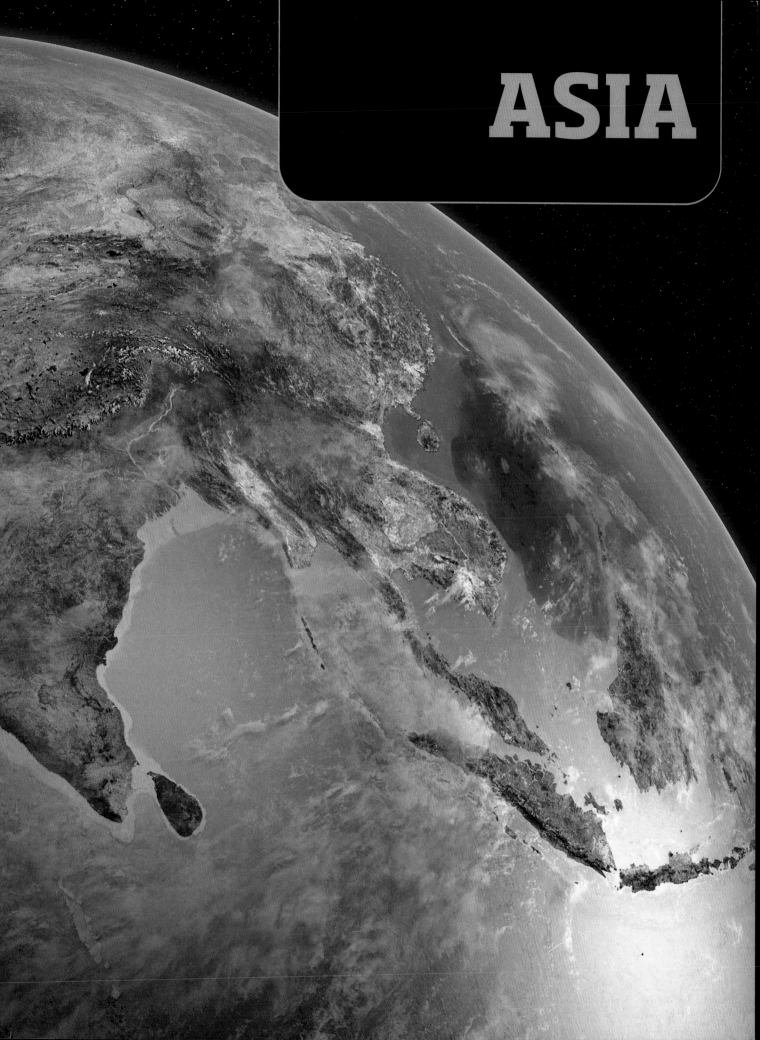

ASIA

Asia

Part of the Eurasian supercontinent with Europe to the west, Asia occupies 30 percent of Earth's land surface. It is also the most people-packed continent, with China and India both home to more than 1 billion residents.

At a glance

Discover some stats and facts about the continent of Asia.

(1) Biggest country by area
Russia, with a total area of 6,601,668 sq miles (17,098,242 sq km), also extends beyond the Ural Mountains into Europe.

(2) Smallest country by area
The Maldives is made up of some 1,200 small coral islands with a total area of just 115 sq miles (298 sq km).

(3) Biggest city by population
Tokyo, Japan, has 14 million residents in the city, and more than 37 million people in the wider metropolitan area.

I don't believe it

The three tallest buildings in the world are in Asia, located in the United Arab Emirates, China, and Saudi Arabia.

How to celebrate Chinese New Year

Chinese New Year is a wonderful 16-day festival celebrating spring. Preparations often begin early, with new clothes bought, houses cleaned, and some redecorated. Many people also light firecrackers.

01. New Year's Eve sees families enjoy a reunion dinner together. Dumplings or sticky cakes are served around midnight, depending on the region.

02. Families honor their elders on New Year's Day and often watch lion or dragon dances (pictured) said to ward off bad spirits.

(4) Biggest lake
The Caspian Sea is bordered by five countries and has a surface area of 149,200 sq miles (386,400 sq km).

(5) Longest river
The Yangtze River, or Chang Jiang, winds its way 3,915 miles (6,300 km) and empties into the East China Sea.

(6) Highest point
Mount Everest is the highest peak in the Himalayas mountain range. Its summit is 29,032 ft (8,849 m) above sea level.

(7) Lowest point
The shoreline of the Dead Sea, located in the Jordan Rift Valley, is 1,410 ft (430 m) below sea level.

The Tsaatan

These Tsaatan people roam isolated stretches of Mongolia, moving to fresh pastures regularly with their reindeer herds and living in tents called ortz. The reindeer are ridden for transportation, used as pack animals, and produce milk for making yogurt and cheese.

Fantastic festivals

Some of Asia's festivals are associated with religion, while others are new and can get pretty muddy!

Holi
This Hindu festival originated in India and celebrates a story of good triumphing over evil. It features dancing and the throwing of brightly colored water and powdered paint.

Boryeong Mud Festival
Rich, mineral mud from South Korea's Boryeong's mud flats are used for messy fun, including big mud slides. This event is popular with locals and tourists alike.

Songkran
This important Buddhist festival in mid-April marks the start of the traditional Thai New Year and involves temple visits, food offerings, and exuberant water fights.

03. The days that follow have their own rituals. On the sixth day, for example, people visit temples and relatives.

04. The fifteenth and last day of New Year is marked by the lantern festival and the lighting of candles to guide wayward spirits home.

Hajj pilgrimage

This annual journey to the holy city of Mecca in Saudi Arabia attracts millions of people every year. It is where the Prophet Muhammad was born, and Islam began. Hajj is a pilgrimage that all Muslims are expected to make at least once during their lifetime.

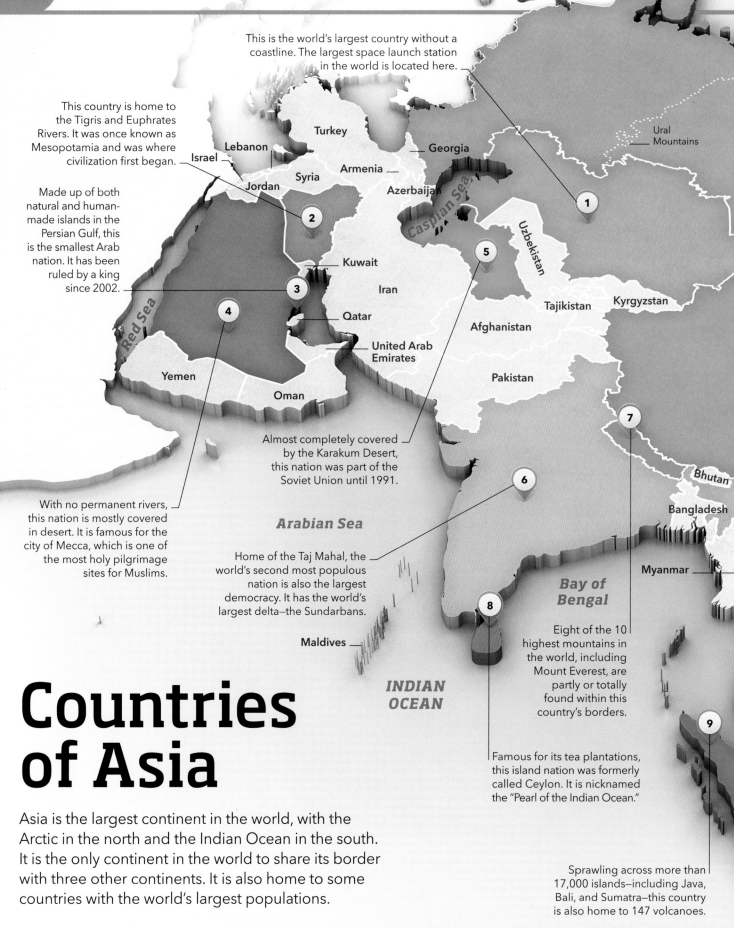

This is the world's largest country without a coastline. The largest space launch station in the world is located here.

This country is home to the Tigris and Euphrates Rivers. It was once known as Mesopotamia and was where civilization first began.

Made up of both natural and human-made islands in the Persian Gulf, this is the smallest Arab nation. It has been ruled by a king since 2002.

With no permanent rivers, this nation is mostly covered in desert. It is famous for the city of Mecca, which is one of the most holy pilgrimage sites for Muslims.

Almost completely covered by the Karakum Desert, this nation was part of the Soviet Union until 1991.

Home of the Taj Mahal, the world's second most populous nation is also the largest democracy. It has the world's largest delta—the Sundarbans.

Eight of the 10 highest mountains in the world, including Mount Everest, are partly or totally found within this country's borders.

Famous for its tea plantations, this island nation was formerly called Ceylon. It is nicknamed the "Pearl of the Indian Ocean."

Sprawling across more than 17,000 islands—including Java, Bali, and Sumatra—this country is also home to 147 volcanoes.

Turkey
Lebanon
Israel
Jordan
Syria
Armenia
Georgia
Azerbaijan
Uzbekistan
Caspian Sea
Kuwait
Iran
Qatar
United Arab Emirates
Afghanistan
Tajikistan
Kyrgyzstan
Pakistan
Yemen
Oman
Red Sea
Ural Mountains
Bhutan
Bangladesh
Myanmar
Maldives
Arabian Sea
Bay of Bengal
INDIAN OCEAN

Countries of Asia

Asia is the largest continent in the world, with the Arctic in the north and the Indian Ocean in the south. It is the only continent in the world to share its border with three other continents. It is also home to some countries with the world's largest populations.

This country occupies one-tenth of all the land on Earth. It also contains the world's longest railway – the Trans-Siberian.

10

Mongolia

North Korea

South Korea

12

PACIFIC OCEAN

11 The most populous country in the world, it has 1.4 billion people and has over 650 cities.

East China Sea

Made up of over 6,800 islands, this country has many active volcanoes, including Mount Fuji, which is its tallest peak.

13 Vietnam

Thailand

Cambodia

South China Sea

This heavily forested nation is crossed by many rivers, including the Mekong, Nam Ou, and Nam Suang.

Taiwan

The island of Borneo is made up of three countries, including this small, oil-rich nation with a population of just 460,000. It is ruled by a sultan.

Malaysia
Singapore

14

Malaysia

Philippines

The newest country in Asia, this tropical, mountainous nation gained independence from Indonesia in 2002.

15

TEST YOURSELF

STARTER
China
India
Indonesia
Japan
Sri Lanka

CHALLENGER
Bahrain
Iraq
Nepal
Russia
Saudi Arabia

GENIUS!
Brunei
East Timor
Kazakhstan
Laos
Turkmenistan

Capital cities

The capital cities of Asia are very varied and include some of the largest in the world. Each has their own unique identity and history. Some have thrived for centuries as centers of trade and power, while others have boomed in modern times.

③ Turkey's second largest city after Istanbul is packed with historic and religious sites, including the Kocatepe Camii Mosque, the largest in the city.

Uzbekistan's largest city is 2,000 years old and is famous for its lively "bazaars" or markets, green spaces, and fountains.

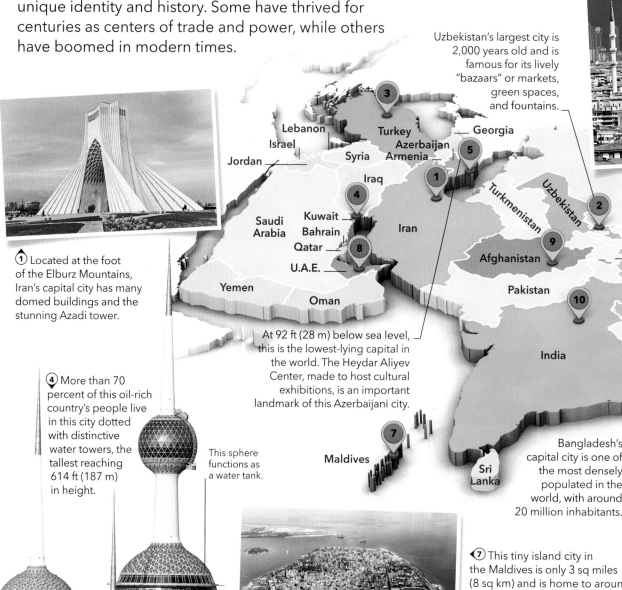

① Located at the foot of the Elburz Mountains, Iran's capital city has many domed buildings and the stunning Azadi tower.

④ More than 70 percent of this oil-rich country's people live in this city dotted with distinctive water towers, the tallest reaching 614 ft (187 m) in height.

This sphere functions as a water tank.

At 92 ft (28 m) below sea level, this is the lowest-lying capital in the world. The Heydar Aliyev Center, made to host cultural exhibitions, is an important landmark of this Azerbaijani city.

Bangladesh's capital city is one of the most densely populated in the world, with around 20 million inhabitants.

⑦ This tiny island city in the Maldives is only 3 sq miles (8 sq km) and is home to around 23,000 residents. It is also a popular tourist destination.

⑧ The spectacular Sheikh Zayed Grand Mosque is located in the heart of the capital city of the UAE.

9 Famed for its ancient palaces, gardens, and religious buildings, the capital city of Afghanistan lies in a valley between the Hindu Kush Mountains.

The 138-ft (42-m) tall India Gate is a war memorial.

10 India's capital was moved from Kolkata to this city situated on the Yamuna River in 1931.

11 The Blue Sky Tower and Sükhbaatar Square are landmarks of the capital city of Mongolia, which is also the coldest in the world.

This statue of revolutionary hero Sükhbaatar stands at the center of the city square.

China's capital is home to 91 universities and the historic palace complex—the Forbidden City.

A statue of the Buddha stands 75 ft (23 m) tall.

13 Ancient Buddhist temples coexist with stunning skyscrapers in South Korea's capital, which has hosted both the Summer and Winter Olympic Games.

Russia

Mongolia **11**

12

China

13 North Korea

Japan

South Korea

Taiwan

Laos

Thailand

Vietnam

15

Cambodia Brunei

Malaysia

Philippines

Indonesia

East Timor

14 A major center of trade in Asia with its large harbor, the capital of the Philippines also contains a historic walled city called Intramuros.

15 Founded in 1434, Cambodia's capital was nicknamed "the pearl of Asia" for its beautiful architecture, including the Royal Palace.

TEST YOURSELF

STARTER
Beijing
Seoul
Ankara
Malé
New Delhi

CHALLENGER
Abu Dhabi
Kuwait City
Kabul
Tehran
Dhaka

GENIUS!
Tashkent
Baku
Phnom Penh
Ulaanbaatar
Manila

ANSWERS: 1. Baku 2. Tashkent 3. Ankara 4. Kuwait City 5. Tehran 6. Dhaka 7. Malé 8. Abu Dhabi 9. Kabul 10. New Delhi 11. Ulaanbaatar 12. Beijing 13. Seoul 14. Manila 15. Phnom Penh

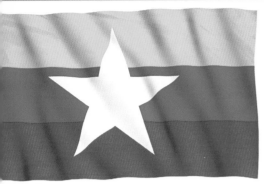

③ ▶ A picture of the Angkor Wat temple decorates the flag of this Southeast Asian kingdom.

② A red circle depicting the Sun represents this country, which is famous for sumo, sushi, and Shinkansen trains.

① Known as Burma until 1989, this country changed its flag in 2010. The white star in the middle of the flag represents the union of the country.

The country is also known as the Land of the Rising Sun.

④ This flag was first flown in 1990, when the north and south of this country on the tip of the Arabian Peninsula were united.

Raise the flag

The flags of Asian nations vary greatly, but they all carry deep historical or religious significance. The world's four tallest flagpoles are all found in this continent, with the tallest in Saudi Arabia, standing 560 ft (171 m) high.

⑤ This small, wealthy nation on the island of Borneo is ruled by a sultan who lives in the world's largest palace, containing 1,788 rooms.

The crescent symbolizes the Islamic faith.

⑥ The lion has been a symbol of this nation for 1,500 years. The green stripe represents its Muslim citizens, the orange Tamil Hindus, and the leaves the four Buddhist virtues.

⑦ The vertical stripe on this Central Asian nation's flag is based on patterns used in the country's traditional carpet weaving industry.

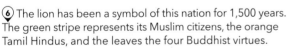

⑧ The flag of this large but sparsely populated country neighboring China has been flown since 1992.

9 The flag of this mountainous kingdom features the Sun and Moon and is the only five-sided national flag in the world.

Red reflects the color of this country's national flower—the rhododendron.

10 Adopted in 1948, this flag belongs to a West Asian country on the Mediterranean.

The six-pointed Star of David is a symbol of the Jewish people.

11 The flag of this Central Asian republic bordering China depicts a birds-eye view of a *yurt*—a traditional tent home.

The 40 rays of sunlight represent the 40 tribes, as well as 40 heroes of this country.

12 The 14 stripes on this flag represent the country's original 13 states plus its capital, Kuala Lumpur.

13 The home of Samsung and K-pop, this high-tech, mostly urban nation shares a peninsula with its northern neighbor.

The spinning wheel is a symbol of Buddhism.

The red-and-blue *yin-yang* symbol represents harmony.

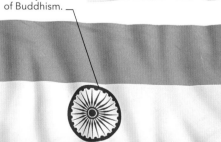

14 More than 1.3 billion people live in this South Asian country, the largest nation in the world where people vote to elect their government.

The "thunder dragon" is white, symbolizing purity.

15 In this small, isolated mountain kingdom, rumbling storms were said to be the roar of *Druk* the thunder dragon, who features on its flag.

TEST YOURSELF

STARTER
- Japan
- Israel
- India
- South Korea
- Malaysia

CHALLENGER
- **Nepal**
- **Bhutan**
- **Cambodia**
- **Sri Lanka**
- **Myanmar**

GENIUS!
- Turkmenistan
- Kyrgystan
- Mongolia
- Brunei
- Yemen

ANSWERS: 1. Myanmar 2. Japan 3. Cambodia 4. Yemen 5. Brunei 6. Sri Lanka 7. Turkmenistan 8. Mongolia 9. Nepal 10. Israel 11. Kyrgystan 12. Malaysia 13. South Korea 14. India 15. Bhutan

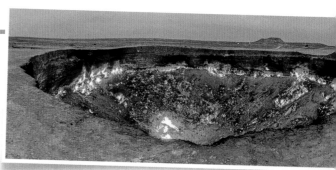

② Nicknamed "The gateway to hell," this fiery pit in Turkmenistan has been blazing continuously since 1971.

① This low-lying body of water on the Israel–Jordan border is 1,410 ft (430 m) below sea level. The world's saltiest stretch of water, swimmers can float easily on its surface.

③ Bizarre-looking dragon's blood trees with red sap dot this isolated island in the Arabian Sea, which is home to more than 600 native species of plants and animals.

This giant salt marsh in the Thar Desert covers an area larger than Israel and shines bright white.

Arabian Sea

INDIAN OCEAN

Bay of Bengal

The highest peak reaches a height of 20,623 ft (6,286 m).

⑤ Located in northern Pakistan, this group of steep rocky peaks and sheer cliffs offer some of the toughest rock-climbing challenges in the world.

Natural wonders

Asia has many incredible natural wonders—from stunning coral reefs to extraordinary rock formations, islands, and waterfalls. How many of these do you recognize?

This native species of land crabs lay their eggs in the Indian Ocean.

⑥ This island is known for the extraordinary spectacle of millions of red crabs scurrying from inland forests to the coast during the mating season each year.

TEST YOURSELF

STARTER	CHALLENGER	GENIUS!
Darvaza Crater	**Tubbataha Reef**	**Mount Kelimutu**
Chocolate Hills	**Kuang Si Falls**	**Socotra Island**
Christmas Island	**Dead Sea**	**Flaming Cliffs**
Mount Fuji	**Trango Towers**	**Zhangjiajie National Forest Park**
Rann of Kutch	**Ha Long Bay**	

7 Found in Mongolia in the middle of the Gobi Desert, these majestic red sandstone canyons and cliffs contain many dinosaur fossils.

8 At 12,388 ft (3,776 m), this world-famous volcano is visible from the Japanese city of Tokyo 60 miles (100 km) away.

9 Surrounded by a dense jungle, this series of waterfalls and shallow turquoise pools can be found in northern Laos.

East China Sea

PACIFIC OCEAN

10 Hundreds of towering pillars in China's Hunan Province rise up to 660 ft (200 m), creating a dramatic landscape that has inspired several sci-fi films.

South China Sea

12 Some 1,600 rocky outcrops and small limestone islands, covered in rainforest, dot the emerald-green waters of this beautiful bay in North Vietnam.

This Indonesian volcano has three crater lakes at its peak, each of which periodically changes color due to volcanic activity.

The grass on each hill turns brown during fall.

13 This rich and colorful coral reef, protected by the Philippines government, is home to more than 350 species of coral and 600 species of fish.

14 A popular tourist attraction, more than 1,250 rounded hills are found in the Bohol region of the Philippines.

Rivers and lakes

Asia is home to the world's largest lake, largest inland sea, and more than 25 rivers that are over 1,242 miles (2,000 km) long. Many of the world's earliest civilizations flourished on the banks of these rivers, which now provide water, food, and transportation links for millions of people across the continent.

① The longest river in southwest Asia flows through Turkey, Syria, and Iraq. Many ancient civilizations, including the Mesopotamian Empire, thrived along its banks.

The historic town of Halfeti in Turkey lies on the eastern bank of this river.

More than 100 rivers flow into Kyrgyzstan's largest lake, which is surrounded by the Teskey Ala-Too mountain range.

③ This is the world's largest inland body of water. Azerbaijan's capital Baku is one of the many settlements located along its coastline.

This once-large lake has been depleted by diverting its waters for farmland. It is now just one-tenth of its size 60 years ago.

Arabian Sea

④ This river flows from the Tibetan Plateau through the cities of Rawalpindi, Karachi, and Mithankot in Pakistan before emptying into the Arabian Sea.

The holy city of Varanasi is situated on the banks of this river.

Bay of Bengal

⑥ Flowing from the Himalayas, this river runs for more than 1,553 miles (2,500 km) before emptying into the Bay of Bengal. This holy river is a place of pilgrimage for Hindus.

This river meets the Zanskar, a major tributary, near Nimmu in northern India.

The Cambodian village of Komprongpok is one of several floating villages on this lake.

⑦ Connected to the Mekong River by a 75-mile (120-km) long waterway, this is the largest freshwater lake in southeast Asia.

TEST YOURSELF

STARTER	CHALLENGER	GENIUS!
Yangtze River	**Mekong River**	**Tonlé Sap**
Ganges River	**Irrawady River**	**Lake Issyk-Kul**
Indus River	**Euphrates River**	**Lake Uvs**
Lake Baikal	**Caspian Sea**	**Shinano River**
	Qiantang River	**Aral Sea**

8 Mongolia's largest lake was once a large inland sea. It is extremely salty and is home to more than 200 bird species.

Two-humped bactrian camels are native to this part of Central Asia.

9 This is the world's largest river lying within a single nation—China. About 3.3 billion tons of cargo travel by ships along its waters every year.

The ice covering this lake during winter can be up to 6½ ft (2 m) thick.

Laptev Sea   *East Siberian Sea*

10 The largest freshwater lake in the world lies in the vast Russian province of Siberia and is 4,797 ft (1,642 m) deep. It contains around one-fifth of the world's river and lake water.

Japan's largest river flows through Nagano and Niigata cities and is 228 miles (367 km) long.

12 This river in China experiences the world's largest tidal bores—powerful waves that can reach a height of 30 ft (9 m).

South China Sea

Nipa palm trees line the banks of this river as it flows slowly through its final stretch in Vietnam.

The Buddhist temple of Wat Arun lies on the banks of this river.

14 Myanmar's most important waterway is named after the Sanskrit word *airāvatī*, which means "elephant river."

13 This river flows through six countries. It is rich in wildlife, including the Siamese crocodile, river dolphins, and freshwater stingrays.

The Himalayas

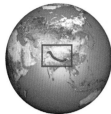

The world's highest mountain range and also one of its youngest, the Himalayas formed about 50 million years ago. They extend more than 1,400 miles (2,300 km) and include more than 100 peaks above 24,000 ft (7,300 m). Few animals are able to survive in this extreme habitat.

① Large and muscular, this plant eater grows a second fur coat over its first to withstand the harsh eastern Himalayan winters.

This is the second-highest peak on Earth.

② This endangered cat is an agile hunter and can survive at altitudes as high as 19,600 ft (6,000 m).

③ Fewer than 400 people have reached the summit of this 28,251-ft (8,611-m) tall peak, often called the "savage mountain" by climbers.

④ This mountain lies partly in India and partly in Nepal. Four of its five peaks are more than 26,247 ft (8,000 m) high. It is the third-highest mountain in the world at 28,169 ft (8,586 m).

The thick tail aids balance.

⑤ Found in forests on the lower slopes, this mammal is a good climber and swimmer. It eats both plants and meat and can weigh up to 397 lb (180 kg).

⑥ The capital city of Bhutan lies in the valley carved by the Raidek River. It is known for its fortified Buddhist monastery and for the fact that its streets have no traffic lights.

8 A little larger than a pet cat, this creature spends most of its time in trees, which it climbs nimbly using its bushy tail for balance.

This iconic square shares its name with the city.

7 Nepal's capital city is filled with Buddhist monasteries and Hindu temples. Many tourists visit this busy city, which is a gateway to the Himalayas.

The tail has distinctive white rings.

9 This large, short-tailed bird of prey soars over the mountains looking for remains of dead animals to eat.

It has a wingspan of up to 3 ft (1 m).

The Bhagirathi River is one of the two rivers that form the Ganges.

10 This bulky animal is found in the wild and is also domesticated. It has thick, long fur and can weigh more than 2,205 lb (1,000 kg).

Its horns can be up to 4 ft (1.2 m) long.

11 This 19-mile (30-km) long river of ice in Uttarakhand, India, is the source of the Ganges River. It is an important pilgrimage site for the Hindus.

Houses are plastered with mud for insulation.

12 Located in Himachal Pradesh, India, this is the highest inhabited settlement in the Himalayas. It lies more than 14,700 ft (4,500 m) above sea level.

14 This wild goat with distinctive curly horns is the national animal of Pakistan. Males have long, light-colored fur on their chest and throat.

13 Towering 29,032 ft (8,849 m) high and rising by about 4 mm every year, the tallest mountain on Earth was first climbed in 1953.

TEST YOURSELF

STARTER	CHALLENGER	GENIUS!
Mount Everest	Kanchenjunga	Markhor
Kathmandu	Thimphu	Takin
Snow leopard	Yak	Komic
Himalayan black bear	Red panda	K2
Gangotri glacier	Himalayan griffon vulture	

Biomes

Twelve of the world's land biomes can be found in Asia. These range from dry deserts, both hot and cold, to warm, wet rainforests and freezing Arctic tundra. This continent is also home to the highest mountain range in the world: the Himalayas.

Types of biomes

- Tropical moist broadleaf forest
- Tropical dry broadleaf forest
- Tropical coniferous forest
- Temperate broadleaf forest
- Temperate coniferous forest
- Desert and dry shrubland
- Temperate grassland and savanna
- Flooded grassland and savanna
- Mediterranean forest and grassland
- Mountain grassland
- Boreal forest
- Tundra

Biomes of Asia

Altindere Valley National Park
Eastern spruce trees grow in this temperate coniferous forest near the Sumela Monastery in Turkey.

Wakhan Corridor
This isolated region in Afghanistan is nestled between three mountain ranges. It stretches for 217 miles (350 km) and includes grasslands and floodplains.

Manyas Bird Paradise
This Turkish national park is filled with willow and tamarisk trees on the shores of Lake Manyas.

Aras Free Zone
This remote area of northwestern Iran averages 59°F (15°C) in the temperate grasslands but gets much colder in the surrounding mountains.

Jiddat al-Harasis
Acacia trees and rock formations dot this sparse desert in Oman. It receives only 2 in (5 cm) of rainfall annually.

Gir National Park
More than 300 bird species and Asiatic lions live in this tropical dry broadleaf forest in India.

Great Himalayan National Park
This high-altitude region includes tropical coniferous forests and is home to the snow leopard.

Animal life

Yak
These sturdy, shaggy mammals have thick fur to survive bitter winters and strong teeth to chew tough mountain grasses.

Himalayan Jumping Spider
Thought to be the highest living animal on Earth, this spider lives in steep mountain slopes as high as 22,301 ft (6,800 m).

Komodo Island

The nutrient-rich waters surrounding this Indonesian national park have more than 1,000 species of tropical fish. They swim through spectacular reefs with 260 different types of coral.

In numbers

46 million sq miles
(12 million sq km) The total area of Russia's boreal forests.

640 miles
(1,030 km) The length of the Caspian Sea, Asia's biggest lake.

24 lb
(11 kg) The weight of a single Rafflesia Arnoldii flower, found in some forests in the Philippines.

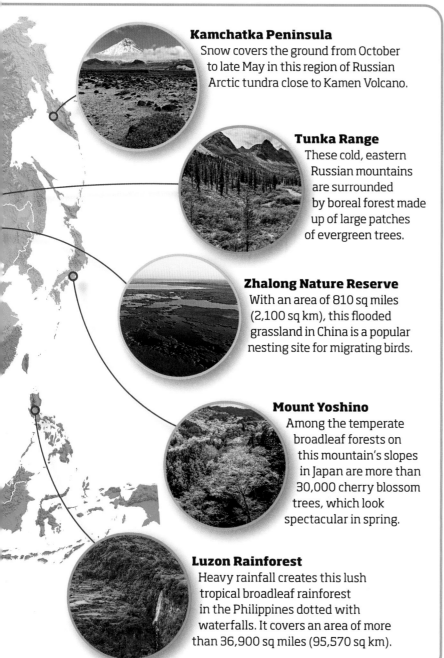

Kamchatka Peninsula
Snow covers the ground from October to late May in this region of Russian Arctic tundra close to Kamen Volcano.

Tunka Range
These cold, eastern Russian mountains are surrounded by boreal forest made up of large patches of evergreen trees.

Zhalong Nature Reserve
With an area of 810 sq miles (2,100 sq km), this flooded grassland in China is a popular nesting site for migrating birds.

Mount Yoshino
Among the temperate broadleaf forests on this mountain's slopes in Japan are more than 30,000 cherry blossom trees, which look spectacular in spring.

Luzon Rainforest
Heavy rainfall creates this lush tropical broadleaf rainforest in the Philippines dotted with waterfalls. It covers an area of more than 36,900 sq miles (95,570 sq km).

Conservation facts

🍃 Breeding programs have seen Mauritius kestrel numbers increase from 6 to 800 in 30 years.

🍃 There are 67 panda reserves across China, protecting both the animal and its habitat.

🍃 To conserve its wildlife, Sri Lanka agreed to quadruple the size of the Sinharja Rainforest in 2019.

1 The males of this South Asian bird display their spectacular tail feathers by fanning them out to attract a female mate.

The tail feathers can be up to 5 ft (1.6 m) long.

2 Asia's largest land animal can weigh up to 12,000 lb (5,400 kg) and eat up to 300 lb (136 kg) of food in a single day!

Its legs can be up to 12½ ft (3.8 m) long.

White spots on its coat aid in camouflage.

3 Also known as the axis deer, this animal is found throughout the Indian subcontinent, living in large herds of 100 or more.

4 The largest crustacean in the world, this creature can grow to the size of a small car and lives in the northwestern Pacific.

Its gray skin is thick but sensitive.

5 This massive mammal found in Nepal and India can weigh up to 5,000 lb (2,200 kg). It has only one horn.

Long fingers help it cling to branches.

6 Each eye of this tiny Southeast Asian primate is as big as its brain and helps it spot insects at night.

7 The largest of the big cats, growing up to 10 ft (3 m) long, is found in India and Bangladesh. An excellent swimmer, it keeps cool in the water on hot days.

It has a distinctive orange coat with black stripes.

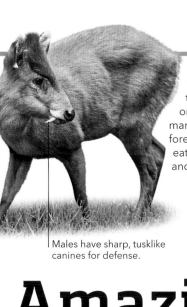

8 Named after the clump of hair on its forehead, this mammal lives in the forests of China and eats grass, twigs, and fruit.

Males have sharp, tusklike canines for defense.

9 Despite weighing up to 180 lb (82 kg), this Southeast Asian primate can move nimbly. It uses its long fingers and toes to peel fruit.

Long arms help it swing from tree to tree.

Amazing animals

Whether it's troops of primates swinging from the trees or the biggest of the big cats prowling through wetlands, animals of all shapes and sizes are found across Asia. This vast continent is also home to many endangered species, such as the giant panda.

Strong fingers are excellent for gripping branches.

TEST YOURSELF

STARTER

Asian elephant
Bengal tiger
Giant panda
Indian rhinoceros
Japanese spider crab

CHALLENGER

Orangutan
Indian peafowl
Japanese macaque
Tufted deer
Gharial

GENIUS!

Chital
Slow loris
Sunda pangolin
Western tarsier

A long snout helps it speed through water.

10 The long, narrow jaws of this South Asian reptile are lined with more than 100 needle-sharp teeth, which interlock to prevent fish from escaping.

Large tail scales help it absorb heat from the Sun or cool down.

Its thick black-and-white coat keeps it warm.

Its large eyes ensure excellent night vision.

11 The only venomous primate in the world is found in Southeast Asia. It is active only at night, when it hunts for small insects.

Its pink face is covered by a very fine layer of fur.

12 Native to central China, this endangered bear feeds almost exclusively on bamboo shoots.

13 When threatened, this Southeast Asian creature can roll up into a hard, scaly ball. It uses its long, sticky tongue to lap up ants and termites.

14 Also known as the snow monkey, this primate keeps itself warm in the mountains of Japan by taking dips in hot springs.

ANSWERS: 1. Indian peafowl 2. Asian elephant 3. Chital 4. Japanese spider crab 5. Indian rhinoceros 6. Western tarsier 7. Bengal tiger 8. Tufted deer 9. Orangutan 10. Gharial 11. Slow loris 12. Giant panda 13. Sunda pangolin 14. Japanese macaque

The structures are 82–160 ft (25–50 m) tall.

2 Extending more than 13,170 miles (21,196 km), this fortification is the world's longest human-made structure.

1 These artificial trees facing Marina Bay in Singapore generate solar electricity, house vertical gardens, and harvest rainwater.

Each clay warrior is clad in military clothing.

4 These two tubes of glass, concrete, and steel in Georgia contain exhibition spaces for music, theater, and art.

3 Hidden inside a narrow gorge in Jordan, this stunning city includes temples and statues carved into the rock face.

The music venue in this part of the building can seat more than 500 people.

5 More than 7,000 life-size statues of soldiers, made around 2,000 years ago, guard the burial complex of Chinese emperor Qin Shi Huang.

Human-made wonders

The world's tallest building, longest fortification, largest mosque, and largest temple can all be found in Asia. The continent is home to many extraordinary architectural achievements—from an ancient city carved into the rock face to artificial trees that can help save water!

The statue is 597 ft (182 m) tall.

7 Rising to a height of 2,716 ft (828 m), this tower in Dubai is the tallest building in the world.

8 Capable of holding up to 2.5 million pilgrims, the world's largest mosque is located in Mecca, Saudi Arabia. At its center lies the shrine, the Ka'bah.

6 Located in Gujarat, this colossal statue of India's first Deputy Prime Minister, Sardar Vallabhbhai Patel, is the tallest in the world. He was responsible for bringing together India's princely states into the Indian Union.

9 Thousands of steps were carved into the mountainsides in the Ifugao province of the Philippines to create these farm fields.

10 Located in Indonesia, the world's largest Buddhist temple has nine platforms, which are decorated with 504 statues of the Buddha.

The combined length of the steps is more than 12,400 miles (20,000 km).

Each tower has 88 stories.

11 Once the world's tallest buildings, these twin structures in Kuala Lumpur, Malaysia, soar to a height of 1,483 ft (452 m).

The dome is typical of the architecture of the Mughal dynasty.

TEST YOURSELF

STARTER
- The Great Wall of China
- Taj Mahal
- Burj Khalifa
- Terracotta Army

12 Carrying six lanes of traffic over the Han River in Da Nang, Vietnam, this crossing is shaped like a fire-breathing monster.

13 Built by Mughal emperor Shah Jahan as the tomb of his wife Mumtaz, this iconic Indian monument is made of marble and sandstone.

CHALLENGER
- Masjid al-Haram
- Petronas Towers
- Dragon Bridge
- Supertree Grove
- Statue of Unity

GENIUS!
- Borobudur Temple
- Banaue Rice Terraces
- Rike Park Concert Hall
- Petra

OCEANIA

Oceania

Oceania covers Australia, New Zealand, and a number of island groups in the Pacific. Some of these countries, including many Oceanic islands, have sandy beaches fringed with beautiful coral reefs.

In numbers

Population
44 million

Size
3,291,903 sq miles
(8,525,989 sq km)

Countries
14

At a glance

Discover some facts and stats about the continent of Oceania.

① Biggest country by area
Australia is much bigger than any other country in Oceania, with an area of 2,941,283 sq miles (7,617,930 sq km).

② Smallest country by area
Nauru is a tiny oval-shaped nation with just one island, measuring 8 sq miles (21 sq km). It is surrounded by a coral reef.

③ Biggest city by population
Sydney, Australia, has 5 million residents in the city, and more than 5.5 million in the wider metropolitan area.

I don't believe it

There are more than 20,000 Pacific islands, which formed when underwater volcanoes erupted to the water's surface.

How to catch a wave

Surfing has been part of Pacific island culture for centuries. Islanders taught visitors to surf, and the sport steadily spread around the world. Here's how it's done–but remember surfing can be dangerous, so always learn with a responsible adult.

01. Find a spot where the waves break as they roll toward the shore. If you're new to surfing, look for small waves and a space where you won't bump into other surfers.

02. Paddle out into the ocean, past the point where the waves break. Keep a lookout to the shore, so you can paddle back in if you feel you are going out too far.

④ Biggest lake
Kati Thanda-Lake Eyre in Australia extends for 3,430 sq miles (8,884 sq km). It is located in a central desert.

⑤ Longest river
The Murray River in Australia is 1,570 miles (2,520 km) long. It flows through three states.

⑥ Highest point
Mount Wilhelm in Papua New Guinea rises 14,795 ft (4,509 m) above sea level and often has snow at its peak.

⑦ Lowest point
Kati Thanda-Lake Eyre in Australia is 49 ft (15 m) below sea level. Usually dry, it is the country's largest salt lake.

The Māori

The Māori are the Indigenous people of New Zealand, with their own unique culture and language. Rawiri Waititi co-leads a political group that represents the Māori people. He is shown here giving a Māori greeting, or "Hongi," with the country's prime minister, Jacinda Ardern.

Australian rules

Australian rules football–or simply "Aussie rules"–is played on an oval-shaped field, with two teams of 18 players. Players aim to score points by kicking a ball through a set of goals made of upright posts.

Now retired, Adam Goodes is one of the greatest players of all time.

03. Lie on your board facing the shore. As a wave carries you forward, push up to standing. Awesome–you're surfing!

04. Keeping your balance is the most important part, but it takes time and patience–and a lot of falling over. With practice, you'll get there!

Fantastic festivals

Oceania has a wide range of festivals, from land-based watersports to daredevil jumping.

Henley-on-Todd Regatta
This race takes place on a dry river bed in Alice Springs, Australia. Teams of runners hold a lightweight boat frame and run around a buoy and back to the finish line.

Te Rā o Waitangi
On February 6 every year, many New Zealanders celebrate the signing of the 1840 Treaty of Waitangi, which is viewed as the founding document of the nation.

Naghol Land Diving festival
Every year, a land diving contest is held on Pentecost Island, Vanuatu. People jump 164 ft (50 m) from a platform with ropes tied around their legs.

Countries of Oceania

This watery continent is made up of three big countries and a collection of thousands of tiny islands, scattered across the Pacific Ocean. Sandy beaches and coral reefs make these islands popular with tourists from all over the world. How many of them can you name?

Philippine Sea

Northern Mariana Islands (to USA)

Guam (to USA)

This nation covers an area of ocean five times bigger than France. Only a tiny part of it is land, in the form of around 600 islands.

4

1

This nation is made up of more than 300 islands. It is known for its stunning coral and reef fish, making it a world-famous diving spot.

Home to the world's third largest rainforest, this country has more than 800 spoken languages.

2

This nation is the size of a continent and the world's largest island. Most of it is desert, known as the Outback, so people mainly live on the coasts.

INDIAN OCEAN

3

TEST YOURSELF

STARTER

Australia
New Zealand
Micronesia
Papua New Guinea

CHALLENGER

Fiji
Marshall Islands
Samoa
Solomon Islands
Tonga

GENIUS!

Kiribati
Nauru
Palau
Tuvalu
Vanuatu

PACIFIC
OCEAN

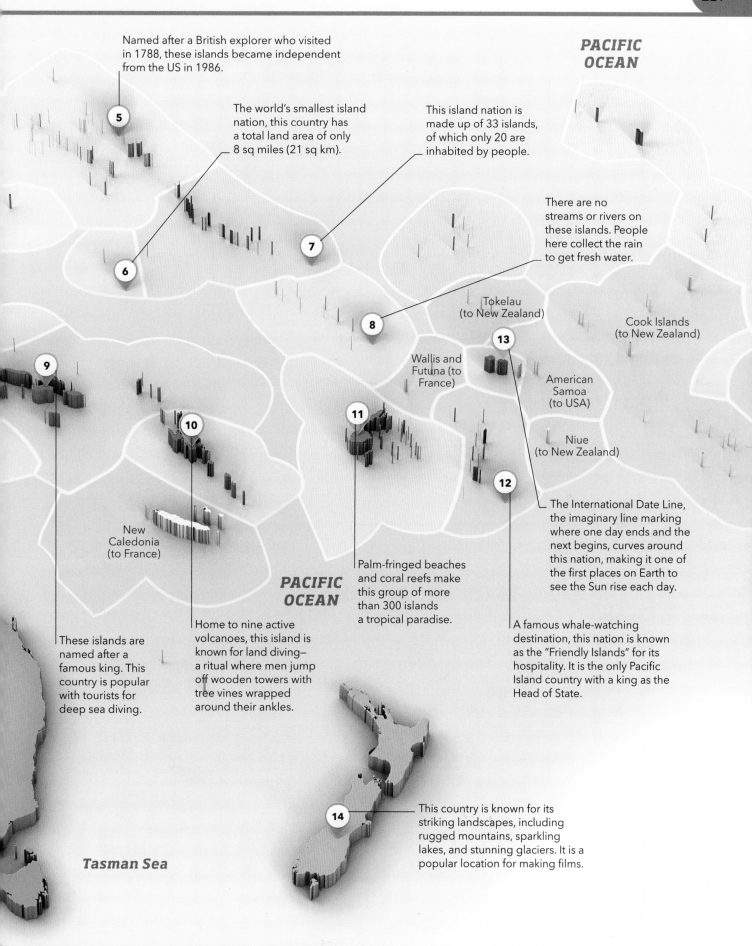

Named after a British explorer who visited in 1788, these islands became independent from the US in 1986.

5

The world's smallest island nation, this country has a total land area of only 8 sq miles (21 sq km).

6

This island nation is made up of 33 islands, of which only 20 are inhabited by people.

7

There are no streams or rivers on these islands. People here collect the rain to get fresh water.

Tokelau
(to New Zealand)

Cook Islands
(to New Zealand)

8

13

Wallis and
Futuna (to
France)

American
Samoa
(to USA)

9

Niue
(to New Zealand)

10

11

12

New
Caledonia
(to France)

PACIFIC
OCEAN

The International Date Line, the imaginary line marking where one day ends and the next begins, curves around this nation, making it one of the first places on Earth to see the Sun rise each day.

These islands are named after a famous king. This country is popular with tourists for deep sea diving.

Home to nine active volcanoes, this island is known for land diving—a ritual where men jump off wooden towers with tree vines wrapped around their ankles.

Palm-fringed beaches and coral reefs make this group of more than 300 islands a tropical paradise.

A famous whale-watching destination, this nation is known as the "Friendly Islands" for its hospitality. It is the only Pacific Island country with a king as the Head of State.

Tasman Sea

14

This country is known for its striking landscapes, including rugged mountains, sparkling lakes, and stunning glaciers. It is a popular location for making films.

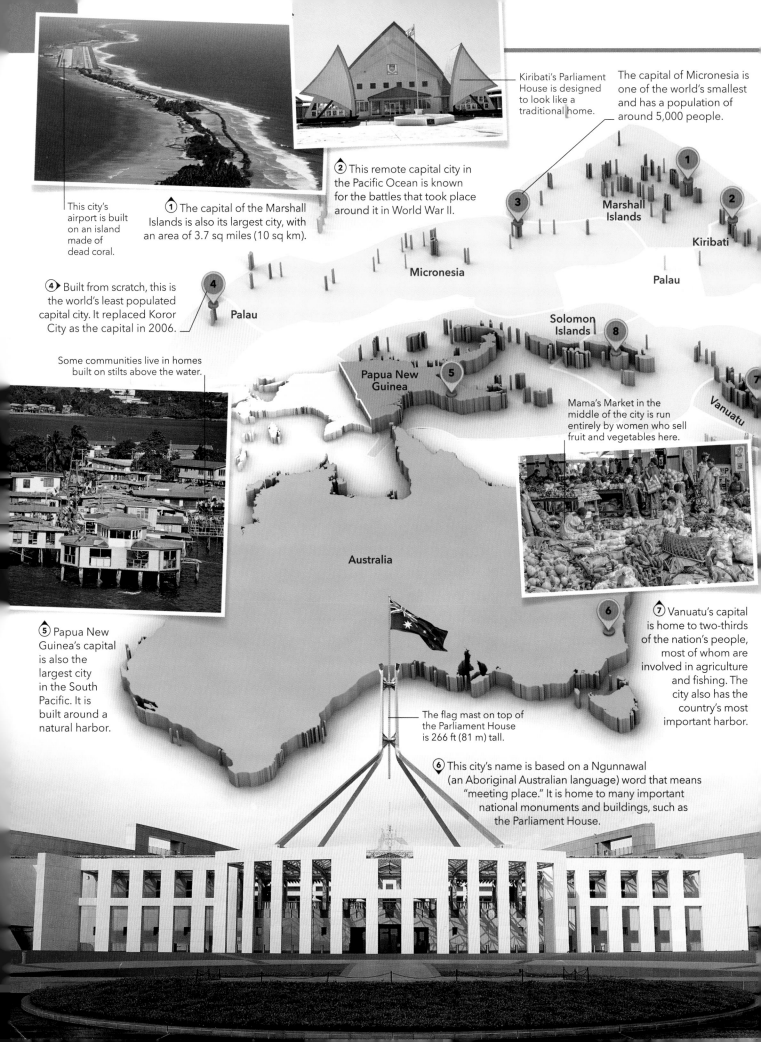

This city's airport is built on an island made of dead coral.

① The capital of the Marshall Islands is also its largest city, with an area of 3.7 sq miles (10 sq km).

Kiribati's Parliament House is designed to look like a traditional home.

The capital of Micronesia is one of the world's smallest and has a population of around 5,000 people.

② This remote capital city in the Pacific Ocean is known for the battles that took place around it in World War II.

Marshall Islands

Kiribati

Palau

Micronesia

④ Built from scratch, this is the world's least populated capital city. It replaced Koror City as the capital in 2006.

Palau

Solomon Islands

Some communities live in homes built on stilts above the water.

Papua New Guinea

Vanuatu

Mama's Market in the middle of the city is run entirely by women who sell fruit and vegetables here.

Australia

⑤ Papua New Guinea's capital is also the largest city in the South Pacific. It is built around a natural harbor.

⑦ Vanuatu's capital is home to two-thirds of the nation's people, most of whom are involved in agriculture and fishing. The city also has the country's most important harbor.

The flag mast on top of the Parliament House is 266 ft (81 m) tall.

⑥ This city's name is based on a Ngunnawal (an Aboriginal Australian language) word that means "meeting place." It is home to many important national monuments and buildings, such as the Parliament House.

8 Located on the island of Guadalcanal, this city contains all the government buildings of the Solomon Islands, including the National Parliament.

The national team has also won the Rugby Sevens World Cup twice.

Around half of Tuvalu's population lives in its capital city, which is located on an island. Rising sea levels are causing it to sink and it may be completely under water in the next 50 years.

9 Fiji's capital is home to a grand sports stadium, which is used by the country's very successful rugby team.

Kiribati

Kiribati

10

Tuvalu

11

Samoa

Fiji **9**

12

Tonga

The city's main fish market is known for its huge variety of freshly caught seafood.

11 This is not just Samoa's capital, but also the only city in the country. It is located on the coast of Samoa's second-largest island, Upolu.

Made of wood, this palace was built in 1867.

12 This capital city houses the Royal Palace, the official residence of the King of Tonga.

13

New Zealand

This body of water is known as the Oriental Bay.

13 This city is the southernmost capital in the world. It is New Zealand's second-largest city, after Auckland.

The iconic cable-run railway connects most of the city's important areas and landmarks.

Capital cities

Most of Oceania's biggest cities are in its largest country, Australia. The continent's island nations generally have much smaller settlements. For some of them, the capital is their only city, while Nauru—the world's smallest island nation—has a total land area of only 8 sq miles (21 sq km) and has no towns or an official capital!

TEST YOURSELF

STARTER
Canberra
Wellington
Tarawa Atoll
Apia

CHALLENGER
Port Moresby
Majuro Atoll
Suva
Ngerulmud

GENIUS!
Honiara
Palikir
Nuku'alofa
Port-Vila
Funafuti Atoll

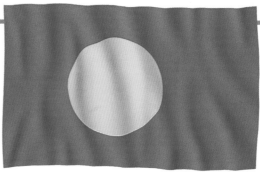

1 Designed by a 15-year-old art student, this flag is inspired by the colors predominantly used in the country's art.

The feathers of the bird of paradise are used in traditional dress.

2 The circle on this flag represents the full Moon, which is a special time of harvest and celebration for the people of this island nation.

3 The red cross represents Christianity, while white symbolizes purity. In 1875, King George Tupou I passed a law stating that the flag's design shall never be changed.

4 Two big islands make up this nation. The Union Jack featured on it represents the country's historic ties with Great Britain.

The white-bordered red stars represent the Southern Cross.

5 More than 600 tiny islands make up this country. The four stars represent island groups and are set against a blue background that symbolizes the Pacific Ocean.

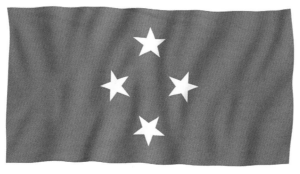

6 This country has two parallel island chains—the Ratak (sunrise) chain is represented by the orange stripe, and the Ralik (sunset) chain by white.

Raise the flag

Oceania is dominated by the Pacific Ocean, and most of the countries here are islands or groups of islands. Many Oceanic flags also feature stars, which link to the Southern Cross—a constellation of stars that can only be seen from the Southern Hemisphere.

7 The color red is used here to symbolize courage. This was the first Pacific island nation to become independent, in 1962.

8 This flag's seven-pointed star refers to this large country's six main states and the final point represents all other territories. The five smaller stars refer to the Southern Cross constellation.

9 This country sits on the equator, surrounded by the Pacific Ocean. Its flag shows the seafaring frigatebird, symbolizing command of the sea.

TEST YOURSELF

STARTER

Australia
New Zealand
Papua New Guinea
Palau

CHALLENGER

Micronesia
Nauru
Marshall Islands
Solomon Islands
Tonga

GENIUS!

Kiribati
Tuvalu
Fiji
Samoa
Vanuatu

10 The blue background symbolizes the Pacific Ocean. The coat of arms features sugar cane, a coconut palm, and bananas, the main agricultural products of this island, as well as a dove of peace.

The boar's tusk symbolizes prosperity.

12 The yellow Y-shape on the flag echoes the pattern in which the country's islands are laid out in the Pacific Ocean.

11 The flag of the smallest country in Oceania shows the country's geographical position, one degree below the equator, which is represented by the gold stripe.

The yellow stripe symbolizes sunshine.

13 The nine stars on this nation's flag stand for its nine islands. Confusingly, this country's name means "eight islands" in the local language.

14 The blue and green colors of this flag signify water and land. The five stars represent the five main island groups, which make up the country.

Natural wonders

Oceania is rich in natural wonders, both on land and underwater. It has rolling deserts and sand dunes, bubbling volcanic features, lush rainforests, and long stretches of untouched coral reefs. Do you know your limestone pillars from your sandstone columns?

① These giant boulders, sacred to the local Aboriginal Australian communities, were shaped by wind and rain wearing away at the rock and earth that surrounded them.

② The world's largest rock is a sacred site for the Anangu people. The rock has a circumference of 6 miles (9 km) and is 1,142 ft (348 m) at its tallest.

Iron in the sandstone gives it an orange-red glow at sunrise and sunset.

Located in Papua New Guinea and part of the Bismarck Range, this is the highest mountain in Oceania at 14,793 ft (4,509 m) above sea level.

Two coral reef barriers protect this area of water from the open ocean. It gets its name from the island that lies at its center.

⑤ Visible from space, this is the largest coral reef in the world. Rising sea temperatures, caused by climate change, are threatening this delicate ocean ecosystem.

Coral Sea

INDIAN OCEAN

More than 1,500 species of fish inhabit the reef.

⑦ One of Australia's best-known landmarks, this group of sea stacks was formed by the continuous erosion of 20-million-year-old limestone cliffs.

Some of these pillars can reach a height of 16 ft (5 m).

⑥ Thousands of limestone pillars rise from the desert in the Nambung National Park in Australia. They take their name from their pointed shape.

Underwater tunnels connect the pool to the ocean.

(9) Every island in American Samoa is surrounded by rings of coral, which provide homes for a huge range of animals, including fish, turtles, and squid.

(10) Mounds of sand dominate the landscape of this national park in Fiji covering an area of 2.5 sq miles (6.5 sq km).

(8) Located on the island of Upolu, Samoa, this swimming hole is 98 ft (30 m) deep. It formed when an ancient volcanic lava tube caved in.

(12) Named after a sparkling drink, this bubbling hot spring in New Zealand has been formed by underground volcanic activity. The water contains toxic minerals, such as sulfur, which make it smell like rotten eggs.

(11) This river of ice flows down New Zealand's Mount Cook. At 15 miles (24 km), it is the largest of its kind in the country.

PACIFIC OCEAN

The water's bright colors are caused by chemical elements in the volcanic rocks.

The pyramid-shaped Mitre Peak is the highest sea-facing cliff in the world.

Many of the rocks are partly buried in the sand.

(13) These large, round rocks dot the coastline of a beach in New Zealand. They are up to 10 ft (3 m) in diameter and can each weigh several tons.

(14) The crystal-clear waters of this 10-mile (16-km) long deep-sea inlet, or fjord, in New Zealand are surrounded by steep cliffs that were carved out by glaciers.

TEST YOURSELF

STARTER

Uluru
Great Barrier Reef
Samoan Coral Reef
The Tasman Glacier
The Twelve Apostles

CHALLENGER

Champagne Pool
Moeraki Boulders
Sigatoka Sand Dunes
Mount Wilhelm
Karlu Karlu/Devils Marbles

GENIUS!

Milford Sound
Marovo Lagoon
To Sua Ocean Trench
The Pinnacles

The U-shaped bend is known as an oxbow.

① The winding bends of this river have often been cut off, forming hundreds of oxbow lakes in the region. It is one of the largest rivers in Papua New Guinea.

② Bright green waterweed on the riverbed can be seen easily through the crystal-clear waters of this river in Papua New Guinea.

③ One of the longest rivers in Australia, its name means "big water" in Wiradjuri, a local Aboriginal Australian language. It is an important source of water for many wetlands.

A heritage railway bridge crosses this river.

Coral Sea

A crust of salt is visible around the lake.

④ Extending for 3,668 sq miles (9,500 sq km), this is Australia's largest lake and lowest point. Surrounded by a desert, this salt lake is often completely dry.

⑤ This is one of the most striking lakes in Australia. The pink color is caused by algae in the water.

INDIAN OCEAN

The shades of pink change throughout the year.

⑥ This is the third longest navigable river in the world at 1,558 miles (2,508 km). The world's largest canoe race is held here each year.

⑦ The deepest freshwater lake in Australia lies in the highlands of Tasmania. It hosts one of the largest fishing competitions in the world.

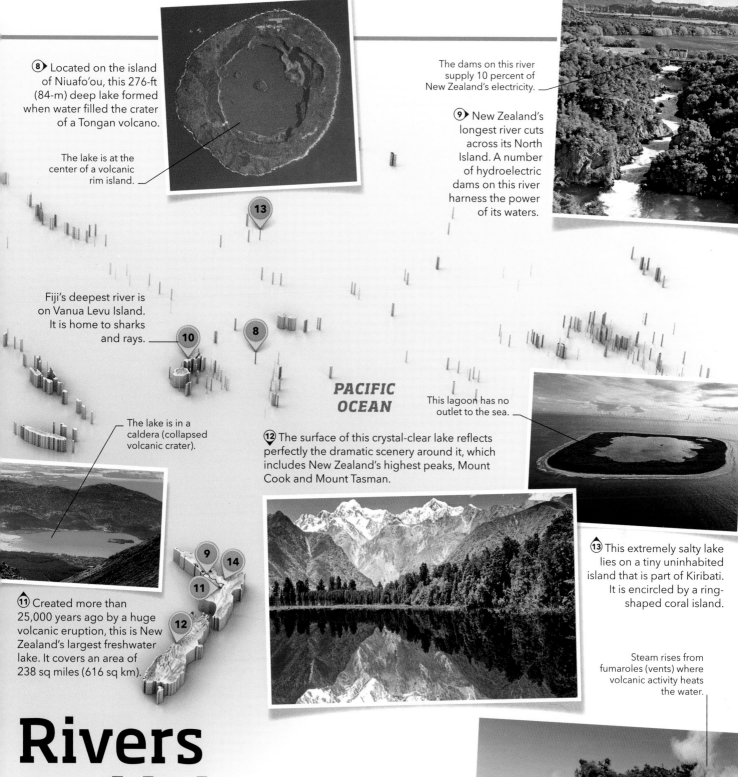

⑧ Located on the island of Niuafo'ou, this 276-ft (84-m) deep lake formed when water filled the crater of a Tongan volcano.

The lake is at the center of a volcanic rim island.

The dams on this river supply 10 percent of New Zealand's electricity.

⑨ New Zealand's longest river cuts across its North Island. A number of hydroelectric dams on this river harness the power of its waters.

Fiji's deepest river is on Vanua Levu Island. It is home to sharks and rays.

PACIFIC OCEAN

This lagoon has no outlet to the sea.

The lake is in a caldera (collapsed volcanic crater).

⑫ The surface of this crystal-clear lake reflects perfectly the dramatic scenery around it, which includes New Zealand's highest peaks, Mount Cook and Mount Tasman.

⑬ This extremely salty lake lies on a tiny uninhabited island that is part of Kiribati. It is encircled by a ring-shaped coral island.

⑪ Created more than 25,000 years ago by a huge volcanic eruption, this is New Zealand's largest freshwater lake. It covers an area of 238 sq miles (616 sq km).

Steam rises from fumaroles (vents) where volcanic activity heats the water.

Rivers and lakes

Many of the island nations that make up Oceania are too small to have large rivers and lakes. Some of them have no rivers or lakes at all! This means that most of the longest rivers in the continent are found on the vast landmass of Australia.

⑭ At the base of Mount Tarawera, New Zealand, this lake is known for its geysers and steaming cliffs. It is also a popular spot for fishing.

Biomes

In Oceania, there are eight biomes on land. While many Pacific islands are covered in rainforest, with coral reefs guarding their coasts, Australia has a vast, dry center that is mainly desert. This continent is rather flat, but New Zealand does have some spectacular mountain terrain.

In numbers

4%
The percentage of Australia that is made up of national parks.

1,500
The age of the oldest tree in New Zealand, called Tāne Mahuta.

1,500
The number of fish species that live in the Great Barrier Reef in Australia.

Biomes of Oceania

Types of biomes

- Tropical moist broadleaf forest
- Tropical dry broadleaf forest
- Temperate broadleaf forest
- Tropical grassland and savanna
- Desert and dry shrubland
- Temperate grassland and savanna
- Mediterranean forest and woodland
- Mountain grassland

Sepik
This tropical broadleaf forest in Papua New Guinea is home to the Sepik River. It is surrounded by rainforests, mountains, and swampy marshes.

Purnululu National Park
Huge striped sandstones–known as the Bungle Bungle Range–reach up to 820 ft (250 m). They are dotted across this tropical grassland and semiarid savanna.

Great Sandy Desert
The Breaden Hills rise up in the Great Sandy Desert that covers 110,040 sq miles (285,000 sq km). Only the toughest animals, such as red kangaroos, can survive here.

Flinders Ranges
The Elder Range in this South Australian area has a Mediterranean climate–cool, wet winters and warm summers. Birds such as emus, parrots, and eagles live in this habitat.

Barrington Tops National Park
Temperate broadleaf forests cover this lush green park with streams weaving through the trees. Owls, bats, and frogs are found here.

Conservation facts

- Elevating the land around Kwajalein Atoll (pictured), Marshall Islands, could help stop the floods caused by climate change.

- In 1964, New Zealand experts introduced the North Island saddleback bird to 19 smaller islands, saving it from extinction.

- Papua New Guinea's largest protected region is a 1,390-sq-mile (3,600-sq-km) forest named Managalas Conservation Area.

Animal life

Across Oceania, animals have adapted to live in their particular biomes. Here are examples from the desert, mountains, and rainforest.

Thorny devil
This lizard is found in Australian deserts. Its spiky body is an excellent defense against predators, but also directs tiny amounts of water to its mouth.

Giant weta
Living in the Southern Alps of New Zealand, this is the heaviest insect in the world, weighing up to 2.5 oz (70 g). In winter, it can freeze solid, then it thaws out in spring.

Crimson-crowned fruit dove
Found in many Pacific islands, from Samoa to Fiji, this tropical bird has green feathers that provide camouflage in its rainforest habitat. It feeds on fruit.

New Caledonia dry forests
By the 1990s, this tropical dry forest was almost completely destroyed due to farming and urbanization on the island, but conservation programs are bringing back life to this habitat.

Aoraki National Park
Steep mountains and spectacular alpine grasslands are the main features of this park in New Zealand. Here, 19 of its peaks are more than 9,800 ft (3,000 m) tall.

Ahuriri River
This 43-mile (70-km) long river is surrounded by temperate grassland containing stretches of beautiful purple lupins. The river itself is full of life, including fish such as rainbow trout.

Mangrove forest

In Palau's Risong Bay, specialized trees can survive at the edges of salty water. Known as mangroves, their roots become a nursery for baby fish and a hiding place for animals escaping predators.

① Loud screeches announce that this small carnivore (meat eater) is nearby. It eats carcasses, as well as hunts live prey.

② Known for its laughing call, this bird is the world's largest kingfisher. It hunts mice, insects, and even snakes!

The tail has stripes or bands running across it.

It has a powerful, broad bill.

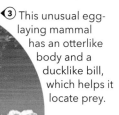

③ This unusual egg-laying mammal has an otterlike body and a ducklike bill, which helps it locate prey.

Webbed toes help this animal pull itself through water.

④ This springy-legged marsupial lives in stony mountain habitats and bounces easily from rock to rock.

Amazing animals

Australia is home to many unique animals that are not found anywhere else in the world. These include many marsupials (pouched mammals), two of the world's three monotremes (egg-laying mammals), and many venomous snakes and spiders. How many can you recognize?

⑤ Australia's largest bird is covered in thick, shaggy feathers. It cannot fly, but has strong legs and massive feet and can run up to 30 mph (48 km/h).

The large, pointed ears help it hear prey, as well as detect danger.

⑦ Watch out for this small but deadly animal! A single bite can cause sickness, sweating, and even death in humans, if left untreated.

⑥ The descendant of domestic dogs that were brought to Australia around 4,000 years ago, this animal lives in the wild and is found all over Australia.

⑧ Often found in wet environments, such as swamps and lagoons, this venomous snake hunts for fish and frogs in shallow water.

ANSWERS: 1. Tasmanian devil 2. Kookaburra 3. Duck-billed platypus 4. Yellow-footed rock wallaby 5. Emu 6. Dingo 7. Redback spider 8. Red-bellied snake 9. Pygmy possum 10. Saltwater crocodile 11. Red kangaroo 12. Sydney funnel-web spider 13. Black-headed python 14. Koala 15. Echidna

9 A long, strong tail acts like a fifth limb and enables this tiny marsupial, just 2½ in (6.5 cm) long, to climb and leap from tree to tree in search of food.

10 Sharp-toothed, scaly, and up to 20 ft (6 m) long, this is the world's largest reptile. It is the only animal in its family that is able to swim in seawater.

Nimble feet are helpful for reaching nectar in flowers.

When threatened, it rears up and displays its fangs.

11 Australia's largest mammal has powerful back legs that allow it to hop across the countryside at speeds of up to 35 mph (60 km/h).

12 Considered to be the deadliest of its kind, this animal uses its huge fangs to stab prey. Its venom can be fatal to humans.

13 This ground-dwelling reptile often hides in hollow logs and rock crevices. It has a varied diet, including small mammals, but seems to prefer eating other snakes.

To sunbathe, this animal only exposes its dark-colored head, which absorbs heat quickly.

14 This animal lives in eucalyptus trees eating their leaves. It sleeps for up to 18 hours a day, gripping onto branches with its long, sharp claws.

The spines provide defense against predators.

15 This spiky, egg-laying mammal uses its long beak to dig up ants and earthworms to eat.

The pouch found only in females helps carry their young, known as joeys.

TEST YOURSELF

STARTER	CHALLENGER	GENIUS!
Red kangaroo	**Pygmy possum**	**Dingo**
Koala	**Red-bellied snake**	**Echidna**
Saltwater crocodile	**Sydney funnel-web spider**	**Tasmanian devil**
Emu	**Kookaburra**	**Yellow-footed rock wallaby**
Redback spider	**Duck-billed platypus**	**Black-headed python**

①▶ Bright and beautiful, this building in Fiji is the largest Hindu place of worship in the Southern Hemisphere.

② This broadcasting tower soars high above the skyline of Auckland, New Zealand. It has three observation decks and restaurants.

The walls are made of volcanic basalt rock.

Human-made wonders

People first arrived in Oceania around 3,000 years ago, and they have been building ever since. The continent is home to ancient statues and sculptures, as well as modern-day structures such as skyscrapers and sports grounds.

③ This ancient city in Micronesia is built around a network of water channels and stands on long columns of volcanic rock, sunk into the coral reef below.

The tower is 1,058 ft (322 m) tall.

◀④ The tallest building in Australia has 78 stories with super-fast elevators that can travel from the ground to the 77th floor in only 42.7 seconds.

⑤ Australia's best-known stadium is named after the sport that was first played here. It can seat more than 100,000 people.

TEST YOURSELF

STARTER

Sydney Opera House
Sky Tower
Melbourne Cricket Ground
Vanuatu Post

CHALLENGER

The Beehive
National Parliament House of Papua New Guinea
Sri Siva Subramaniya Temple

GENIUS!

Ha'amonga 'a Maui
Tjibaou Cultural Centre
Q1 building
Nan Madol
Easter Island Moai

6 Legend has it that these three stones in Tonga were set up this way by the demigod Maui—because no human would have had the strength to lift them.

Each structure is inspired by the traditional houses of Kanak chiefs.

7 Sail-shaped "shells" make up the roof of this instantly recognizable building, which is a performing arts center in Australia.

8 This government building is designed to look like a grand version of one of its traditional houses of worship.

10 New Zealand's parliament building is 236 ft (72 m) tall and houses the office of the country's prime minister.

9 A cultural center in New Caledonia, these buildings celebrate the traditions of its Indigenous Kanak people.

The building is designed to look like a traditional woven bee basket, called a "skep."

The mailbox is 10 ft (3 m) underwater, in Mele Bay.

11 Opened in 2003, this is the world's only underwater post office. It is fully functional, and a flag raised above a float signals if it is open.

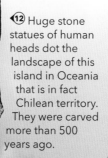

The statues are believed to represent the ancestors of the ancient Polynesians.

12 Huge stone statues of human heads dot the landscape of this island in Oceania that is in fact Chilean territory. They were carved more than 500 years ago.

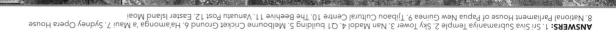

Index

Acknowledgments

The publisher would like to thank the following people for their help with making this book: Ann Baggaley for proofreading; Elizabeth Wise for indexing; Nidhilekha Mathur and Vicky Richards for editorial assistance; Aparajita Sen for making illustrations; Vagisha Pushp for picture research assistance; Shanker Prasad for technical assistance; and Adam Brackenbury for helping out with CGI rendering.

Picture Credits

The publisher would like to thank the following for their kind permission to reproduce their photographs:

(Key: a-above; b-below/bottom; c-center; f-far; l-left; r-right; t-top)

123RF.com: Ekaterina Belova 75tr, carmengabriela 85b, Janice Chen 56tr, emelphoto 128tl, Dirk Erckenf 82br, San Hoyano 74cb, ikachan 100tl, jakobradlgruber 32crb (Sandstone), Mariusz Jurgielewicz 33clb (Falls), Konstantin Kalishko 140cl, Aleksandra Kossowska 97tl, Andrea Marzorati 105tl, Vladimir Melnikov 33crb, mtellioglu 39tr, Erlantz Perez Rodriguez 83cb, saiko3p 75bl, 84bl, Nico Smit 100cla, Donovan van Staden 104bl, Johan Swanepoel 100-101tc; **4Corners:** Reinhard Schmid 140tl, Richard Taylor 30br; **Alamy Stock Photo:** Peter Adams Photography 12crb, agefotostock 12tr, agefotostock / Dave Stamboulis 102cl, / Eric Baccega 103br, / Juan Carlos Muñoz 81ca, / Pablo Méndez 125cra, Coşkun Akşekerci 146cl, All Canada Photos 79cla, Sally Anderson 154-155b, Arcaid Images Renzo Piano Building Workshop and ADCK 171c, Arctic Images 28crb, Rob Arnold 20-21b, Art Directors & TRIP 13cla, Arterra Picture Library / van der Meer Marica 93crb, Auscape International Pty Ltd 140br, Sergio Azenha 122br, Stuart Black 66crb (Gaucho), blickwinkel 4bc, 19cla, 19crb, blickwinkel / A. Hartl 127cb, Blickwinkel / Agami / D. Shapiro 81cra, blickwinkel / D. Mahlke 126ca, Elena Bobrova 88crb, Levente Bodo 136cb, Joerg Boethling 21ca, Karim Bouchetata 41cb, Marc Bruxelle 44cr, John Cancalosi 25ca, Cavan Images / CI2 59cla, Dennis Cox 35clb, CPA Media Pte Ltd / Pictures From History 41cr, Janos Csernoch 49cb, Rachid Dahnoun 58clb (Trees), Danita Delimont / Andres Morya Hinojosa 103clb, David Tipling Photo Library / david tipling 60br, dbtravel 62cr, Phil Degginger 23cl, Reinhard Dirscherl 158cl, DOD Photo 16bc, Dukas Presseagentur GmbH / Prisma / Raga Jose Fuste 92cla, Peter Eastland 125tl, Richard Ellis 44crb (Dancers), ephotocorp / Ashish Kothari 146br, ephotocorp / Hrishikesh Karandikar 168crb, Colin Harris / era-images 18clb, Greg Balfour Evans 128ca, Michele Falzone 75crb, 151cb, 175bl, fletchjr 76cl, FLPA 60crb, Kevin Foy 133cr, funkyfood London - Paul Williams 2ca, 122cla, Galaxiid 165cr, Vlad Ghiea 53tl, Tom Gilks 99tr, Granger Historical Picture Archive 28cl, Glenn Gregory 124clb (Teutoburg), Guy Edwardes Photography 126tl, Mario Gyß 76tr, Gavin Hellier 136bl, Gavin Hellierf 107cl, Hemis 70bc, Hemis.fr / Franck Guiziou 66crb, Hemis.fr / Louis-Marie Preau 88crb (Sahara), Hemis.fr / Sylvain Cordier 82ca, Hemis.fr / Vincent Prevost 155br, HEYL Collective 124bl, Ian Dagnall 93tc, Image Professionals GmbH 76bl, 141br, imageBROKER 49tl, 77ca, 141bc, 143tl, 159cb, imageBROKER / Florian Kopp 66cr, / Frank Sommariva 127cl, / Manfred Schmidt 111br, / Moritz Wolf 167bl, incamerastock 99bc, infocusphotos.com / Malie Rich-Griffith 166ca, INSADCO Photography / Martin Bobrovsky 30crb, Interfoto 57cb, 172t, Chris Ison 167cra, ITAR-TASS News Agency / Vladimir Smirnov 21tc, ITPhoto 170cb, Jan Jerman 163tr, Madeleine Jettre 67t, John Warburton-Lee Photography 137cla, Inge Johnsson 54cl, prabhjit s kalsi 142clb, Foad Karos 98cl, Afzal Khan 35cb, Andrey Khokhlov 125clb (Kalmykia), 125bl, Dorling Kindersley ltd 122crb, Alexey Kornylyev 147bl, Eric Lafforgue 89t, LatitudeStock 55crb, Thomas Lehne 13tr, 173tc, Chavalit Likitratcharoen 56c, Imaginechina Limited 35tr, Cro Magnon 75tc, Markus Mainka EMAAR ENTERTAINMENT 151clb, Dirk Daniel Mann 125crb, mauritius images GmbH 120br, Neil McAllister 93ca, Angus McComiskey 164br, Media Drum World 29bl, 31crb, 40tc, 118tl, Mic Clark Photography 148cl, John Michaels 124cl, Hercules Milas 146cla, Minden Pictures 34tl, 54tl, 97ca, 99br, 104tl, Minden Pictures / BIA / Alan Murphy 60-61t, / Mark Moffett 167cr, / Mike Parry 169tr, Mira / MiraMira 52cla, 174bl, Brad Mitchell 56tl, MJ Photography 92b, Eric Nathan 93br, National Geographic Image Collection / Joel Sartore 126crb, Nature Picture Library 14clb, 15br, 36tr, 57bl, Nature Picture Library / Nick Garbutt 147br, Newscom / BJ Warnick 61cla, Victor Nikitin 147c, Roger Norman 166clb, Michael Patrick O'Neill 147tr, Andrea Obzerova 30ca, Ingo Oeland 31clb, Paulo Oliveira 37tc, Evelyn Orea 44crb, orhandurgut 133br, PA Images / Niall Carson 111cra, Panther Media GmbH / zatletic 111crb, Edward Parker 78tr, Dimple Patel 171tl, Sean Pavone 150tl, Gerry Pearce 169ca, photostaud 146bl, PhotoStock-Israel 24clb, Alexander Piragis 147cla, PjrStudio 24ca, 173bl, Png Studio 63tr, Prisma by Dukas Presseagentur GmbH 99c, Francesco Puntiroli 5cra, 149t, Muhammad Mostafigur Rahman 15bl, Morley Read 79tr, David Reed 24-25, Edward Reeves 15crb, Juergen Ritterbach 84br, robertharding 14cl, 55bl, 70cla, National Parliament of Papua New Guinea 171cra, robertharding / Last Refuge 74tr, robertharding / Michael Nolan 45tl, Robertharding / Michael Runkel 62tc, 92tc, Juan Carlos Muñoz Robredo 78tl, Prasit Rodphan 111cr, Erlantz Pérez Rodriguez 80br, ronnybas 162bc, Guido Schiefer 122bl, Alex Schleif 16tr, Malcolm Schuyl 127crb (Butterfly), Science History Images 28tl, Science Photo Library / Alberto Ghizzi Panizza 84tl, Christopher Scott 93bl, 106tr, Phil Seale 14tr, Paris Spellson 41br, Jose Luis Stephens 85tl, DerbySusan / Stockimo 70bl, Nephatiu / Stockimo 37c, Ozzcam / Stockimo 164clb, Stocktrek Images, Inc. 28clb, Víctor Suárez 146bc, Tierfotoagentur / D. M. Sheldon 125cr, Darya Ufimtseva 28br, Tom Uhlman 59cb, Marek Uliasz 58cla, Universal Images Group North America LLC / DeAgostini 102clb, Genevieve Vallee 166br, Ivan Vdovin 106cl, 142cla, Juan Vilata 58bl, VWPics / Jimmy Villalta 74tl, David Wall 165tr, 170crb, Chris Wallace 145tr, JJ Walters 59cb (Lake), WaterFrame_fba 125br, Dave Watts 127c, 168cla, 169tl, Westend61 GmbH / Alun Richardson 147tl, WILDLIFE GmbH 124clb, Jan Wlodarczyk 114cra, 150cra, Xinhua / Liu Jigang 132-133b, Xinhua / Wang Kai 147cb, Ariadne Van Zandbergen 99cla, Zoonar GmbH 12bl, Zoonar GmbH / Eugen Haag 103tc (lemur), ZUMA Press, Inc. / Ringo Chiu 40cla; **Clerk of the House of Assembly in Kiribati:** 158tc; **AWL Images:** Karol Kozlowski 49cra; **Glenn Banks:** 164tc; **H.E., N.E. Zimmermann, T.R. McVicar, N. Vergopolan, A. Berg, E.F. Wood: Present and future Köppen-Geiger climate classification maps at 1-km resolution, Scientific Data 5:180214, doi:10.1038/sdata.2018.214 (2018).:** 12-13c; **Courtesy of Nakheel:** 35ca; **Depositphotos Inc:** a.new295@gmail.com 151cra, abriendomundo 170-171b, Blackdiamond67 60tl, MagicBones 99cra, photonatura 34br, richie0703 150-151b, vlade-mir 107cla; **Dorling Kindersley:** Terry Carter Uluru-Kata Tjuta National Park 162cla, Harry Taylor / Natural History Museum, London 25crb, Colin Keates / Natural History Museum, London 24tl, 25cra, Natural History Museum, London / Tim Parmenter 22tl, Oxford University Museum of Natural History / Gary Ombler 4ca, 22crb; **Dreamstime.com:** 10tr, 39cb, 129tl, Ajdibilio 40tl, Albertoloyo 120cra, Anton Aleksenko 92tr, Alexpro9500 123tc, Mehriban Aliyeva 123tr, Steve Allen 171tc, Ambientideas 3cla (X2), 60clb, Anankkml 168bl, Brett Andersen 162tl, Leonid Andronov 62b, 120ca, 136cra, Apartura 39fclb, Atosan 79c, Kushnirov Avraham 77clb, Axel2001 119tc, Rui Baião 75cra, BiancoBlue 163bc, Mikhail Blajenov 105tc, Ivanka Blazkova 127cla (Butterfly), Blueringmedia 20cra, Igor Boldyrev 145crb, Jacob Boomsma 54cb, Pichit Boonhuad 21tl, Katrina Brown 52cb, Krzysztof Bubel 22cb, Mariusz Burcz 39tc, Byelikova 17tl, 55tl, 77tl, Casanowe 141cra, Sheryl Caston 38fcrb, Richie Chan 120cl, Chrismrabe 82tl, Dmitry Chulov 19tl, Colette6 149tl, Daboost 96clb, Delstudio 107c, Demerzel21 92cl, Derejeb 93tl, Dimbar76 115tc, Doethion 67br, Wayne Duguay 19cra, Duskbabe 23t, Erectus 38cb, Lane Erickson 20ftr, Inger Eriksen 19br, Alexandre Fagundes De Fagundes 71tl, Farinoza 83ca, Carolyn Franks 57tc, Janos Gaspar 121clb, Gilitukha 148tr, 172bl, Ben Goode 164crb, Marilyn Gould 60bl, Karen Graham 162br, Gerold Grotelueschen 143bl, Vera Gummesson 123cl, Hel080808 79b, Henkbogaard 2ca (Bird), 126tr, Melanie Hobson 97cr, Martin Holverda 10cra, Hotshotsworldwide 54bl, Isselee 5tl, 61tc, 105tr, 127tc, 144cr, 168tc, Barbara Jagosz 39cb (cloud), Jaysi 115cra, 115bl, Jmrocek 127bc, Johncarnemolla 21tc (Uranium), Kaycco 149bc, Linda Kennard 163cra, Kunal Khurana 137tc, Miroslaw Kijewski 78clb, Kingofswords 103tc, Raimond Klavins 145cr, Kmiragaya 4tc, 48tr, 48br, Michal Knitl 17cra, Kjetil Kolbjornsrud 103tr, Sergii Kolesnyk 98tr, 121cr, Laszlo Konya 158cr, Geoffrey Kuchera 60l, Matthijs Kuijpers 169cr, Alain Lacroix 20tc (Sun), Lateci 123br, Pierre Leclerc 120tl, Liz Lee 143tc, Magann / Markus Gann 10tl, Anastasiia Malinich 127tl, Dmitry Malov 159cra, 170cra, Marabelo 144cla, Marcorubino 128bl, Maurizio De Mattei 80bl, Sergey Mayorov 96tl, 96cla, 175tr, Olga Mendenhall 63cb, 173br, Milkakotka 148cra, Minnystock 128bc, Martin Molcan 33clb, Dmitriy Moroz 24tr, Luciano Mortula 4cra, 63tl, Mrincredible / Torian Dixon 10ca, MrLis 100ca, Tomas Nevesely 3bl, 16cla, Niserin 114cl, Nmint 38clb, Duncan Noakes 5cb, 168tr, Boonlong Noragitt 118clb, Notistia 129cr, Serge Novitsky 170tr, Elena Odareeva 136cla, Christian Offenberg 106cb, Jason Ondreicka 59cr, Outdoorsman 19clb, Paddyman2013 21ftl, Pancaketom 38cb (cloud), Sean Pavone 49b, Percent 38clb (cloud), Photographerlondon 61cl, Photonewman1 145ca, Dmitry Pichugin 96tr, Pipa100 122tl, Steven Prorak 38crb, Mariusz Prusaczyk 98clb, José Luis Raota 77bl, Matyas Rehak 70tr, 140tr, Reinhardt 33crb (Glacier), Revenaif 127cla, Manon Ringuette 48tl, Rodrigolab 54tr, Dmitry Rukhlenko 145cl, Saiko3p 74-75cb, 77br, 120bl, Scol22 4tl, 11cr, Richard Semik 128tc, Sfmthd 84cra, Anthony Shaw 137br, Slaviyanka 5ca, 123bc, Hans Slegers 149fbr, Slowmotiongli 126tc, Graeme Snow 159tl, Rakonjac Srdjan 141crb, Lawrence W Stolte 20tr, Tariq Hameed Sulemani 140crb, Parinya Suwanitch 22b, Swallace5 168tl, Tagore75 123c, David Taljat 118c, Baramee Temboonkiat 32crb, Tianshun 158tl, Tifonimages 77crb, Aleksandar Todorovic 142crb, Tomas1111 128cr, Anibal Trejo 107tc, Troichenko 127crb, Tt 15tc, Marek Uliasz 123clb, Urospoteko 127cr, Vnikitenko 39clb, S Walker 39crb, Watink 5tr, 149tr, Saowakon Wichaichaleechon 3cra, 61tr (tree), Wirestock 106crb, Wrangel 12cra, Wrangel 148ca, Björn Wylezich 22tc, Wim Wyloeck 144tr, Xbrchx 34cr, 119cb, Michael Zysman 79cr; **Getty Images:** Martin Tengelin / 500px 97crb, AFP / Dirk Waem 67clb, AFP / NHAC NGUYEN 31tc, AFP / Stan Honda 63cl, AFP / Stringer 159tr, Vanuatu Post Limited 171cl, DANIEL SLIM / AFP 58clb, Andrew Stranovsky Photography 144crb, Barcroft / Contributor 37tl, Ingólfur Bjargmundsson 28tc, Robert Cianflone 155tr, John Coletti 49crb, Matteo Colombo 144-145b, Corbis / Reinhard Dirscherl 167br, Corbis Documentary / Maremagnum 31cla, Alessandro Dahan / Contributor 18cla, DigitalVision / Jordan Siemens 58crb, DigitalVision / Walter Bibikow 59c, DoctorEgg 141tr, E+ / Onfokus 58cra, / Phooey 2cl, Education Images / Contributor 14crb, ElOjoTorpe 71c, EyeEm/ Andrea Savoca Andrea Savoca 29tr, / Fabian Plock 89bl, / Friederike Knauer 59cla (Iceberg), / Guillaume Carnet 167ca, Hafizal Talib / 151c, / Igor Kudryashov 5ca (Mountain), 119c, / Yus Iran 29crb, fmajor 2cla, 106-107b, Robert_Ford 58br, Rodrigo Friscione 34cla, Earl Gibson III / Contributor 49cla, Patrick_Gijsbers 101cl, Fiona Goodall 155crb, guenterguni 96br, by Marc Guitard 57tl, 57ca, John Philip Harper 17clb (Ice), Péter Hegedűs 126cla, Helifilms Australia 40clb, Hagen Hopkins 155tl, The Image Bank / Kevin Schafer 81crb, / Mark Newman 62cra, / Martin Harvey 102crb, / Mary Ann McDonald 100cr, / Tuul & Bruno Morandi 133tl, imageBROKER / Florian Bachmeier 146cra, / Juergen & Christine Sohns 169crb, Tetra Images 53cra, ImaZinS / helloyoungjin 100tc, Johnny Johnson 18b, Chung Sung-Jun 133cra, Layne Kennedy 25tr, 76crb, Mark Kolbe 163tl, Mark Kolbe / Staff 159c, Oleksandra Korobova 32cb, Loïc Lagarde 165cb, Danny Lehman 45b, 56crb, LightRocket / SOPA Images / Tamal Shee 133tr, Ricardo Lima 78c, Jacob Maentz 141tl, Photo by Claude-Olivier Marti 119clb, Joe McDonald 105bl, Moment / © Juan Carlos Vindas 83br, Moment / © Santiago Urquijo 88cr, Moment / Alexandre Morin-Laprise 81c, Moment / Angel Villalba 102cla, Moment / AtomicZen 81cr, Moment / Brandi Mueller 167tl, Moment / by wildestanimal 80cla, Moment / Dave Carr 59bc, Moment / Douglas Klug 59tr, Moment / Gianfranco Vivi 62tl, Moment / Istvan Kadar Photography 45tc, Moment / Jean-Philippe Tournut 146clb, Moment / John White Photos 166c, Moment / Maiquel Jantsch 80crb (Huascaran), Moment / Renan Gicquel 80crb, Moment / Roberto Machado Noa 63bl, Moment / Wei Hao Ho 162crb, 167clb, Moment Open / Celso M. Kuwajima 84cr, Moment Open / totororo 147cb (Yoshino), Moment Unreleased / Pink Pixel Photography 129cb, Arlan Naeg / Stringer 29cr, Nico De Pasquale Photography 29cla, Peter Pokrovsky 148clb, Posnov 30tl, Mike Powles 149br, REDA&CO / Universal Images Group Editorial 17clb, Robert Ross 96cb, Sian Seabrook 30bl, Max shen 164bl, Abhishek Singh 148b, STF / Staff 34tr, Stone / Georgette Douwma 103ca, Oliver Strewe 15cla, Keren Su 143cb, TASS / Ilya Timin 125clb, TASS / Lev Fedoseyev 111tl, 124cr, Wendell Teodoro 155cr, The Image Bank / Robin Smith 16bl, Universal Images Group / Education Images 81cra (sloth), / View Pictures / Hufton+Crow 107cra, / VW Pics / Andre Seale 163ca, / VW Pics / Federico Tovoli 110-111b, Universal Images Group Editorial / BSIP 60tc (X6), Luis Vera / Stringer 71tc, Volanthevist 105cla, Westend61 37b, 70crb; **Getty Images / iStock:** aimintang 52clb, Andreygudkov 105crb, aphotostory 141cr, aprott 53c, Claudio Arriagada 81bl, benedek 38c, BenGoode 38fclb, Bobbushphoto 14fcrb, bogdanhoria 38cl, Bombaert 63ca, brytta 13crb, cinoby 63br, Danielrao 145cb, Don Donelson 14cla, E+ / apomares 80cra, / brittak 89crb, / DieterMeyrl 126b, / Edsel Querini 81clb, / Gerald Corsi 101tr, / mollypix 17bc, / Phooey 129tr, / powerofforever 114tc, / robas 21r, / RollingEarth 81cla, / rusm 5bl, 115tl, 163cb, / Sjo 167crb, / THEPALMER 83bl, ferrantraite 56bc, Robert_Ford 12cla, Gannet77 25tl, Gargolas 129ca, GlobalP 5br, 169cb, Goddard_Photography 137cra, Angel Gruber 71b, guenterguni 13ca, 97bl, 98crb, 103cl, HannesThirion 13bl, Ray Hems 35cb (Iceberg), IvancoVlad 105ca, ivkuzmin 78bc, Dominic Jeanmaire 168bc, JeremyRichards 16cl, barmah john 164c, kaphotokevm1 100-101b, kokkai 158b, Ajith Kumar 2cb, 52tc, Luckohnen 76cb, Mlenny 19tc, Model-la 2c, 23cra, mtcurado 96crb, narvikk 142cb, nattanan726 105c, neirfy 115cb, nodramallama 53bl, orpheus26 137crb, paulafrench 104cr, pawel.gaul 114b, ph2212 99crb, Prakich 16crb, prmustafa 151tc, reptiles4all 82cl, Juergen Sack 136br, SeanPavonePhoto 31c, Shalinder Sharma 144cb, Grant Thomas 104tr, TomasSereda 128-129c, ugniz 149bl, 174br, sara_winter 12cl, wwing 25c; **Marius Jovaisa photo from the album "Unseen Cuba":** 55cr; **NASA:** Image courtesy of the Earth Science and Remote Sensing Unit, NASA Johnson Space Center 165tc; **naturepl.com:** Heather Angel 15tr, Franco Banfi 57crb, Suzi Eszterhas 83tr, Shane Gross 34ca, Pascal Kobeh 18cra, Gavin Maxwell 147tc, Alex Mustard 36br, Terry Whittaker 104crb, Rod Williams 83cr; **Ocean Exploration Trust:** 36bl; **BAS:** Antony Dubber 18ca; **Robert Harding Picture Library:** Yoshio Tomii Photo Studio 85c; **Science Photo Library:** Bernhard Edmaier 74cla, MSF / Javier Trueba 30cb; **Robbie Shone:** 31cra; **Shutterstock.com:** 1WorldTravels 143crb, Jody Ann 61clb, Artush 103bl, BearFotos 148tl, Yevgen Belich 171cr, Uwe Bergwitz 78crb, Neil Bowman 127cra, Natalya Bozadzhy 119cra, Carl DeAbreu Photography 3tr, 61tr, cellistka 4br, 82-83t, Amos Chapple 41tr, Conservationist 149clb, John Crux 55clb, danm12 40-41b, Denzel9 120tc, Designua 26clb (x3), Oleg Dimitrov 121tl, Vorobyev Dmitry 99tl, Dobermaraner 83tc, Nejdet Duzen 142tr, EastVillage Images 101cra, U. Eisenlohr 20tc, EpicStockMedia 52br, Evdokim Eremenko 101tc, Fotos593 82b, iacomino FRiMAGES 35br, 118br, Reziel Gatchalian 151ca, Globe Guide Media Inc 36cl, Evgeny Gorodetsky 165clb, graphia 30tr, Ken Griffiths 168br, Keith Hider 114clb, HPK Images 85ca, idiz 168-169c, Eric Isselee 127clb, Eric Isselee 149cb, Joanna Rigby-Jones 97tr, Ruslan Kalnitsky 163bl, Venera Koiava Doriana and Massimiliano Fuksas 150ca, A_Lesik 35tl, Photographer Lili 33cb, LizCoughlan 170tc, Harald Lueder 120cb, Janelle Lugge 164cra, Kunal Mahto 151tl, Martchan 106cra, Sidoine Mbogni 106clb, MD_Photography 102br, Martin Mecnarowski 60bc, Angela Meier 85cla, Vladimir Kogan Michael 126cl, N Mrtgh 13crb (spinifex), R.M. Nunes 76br, Manuel Ochoa 71crb, Herbert Meyrl / Westend61 on Offset 36cb, Augusta Oosthuizen 16br, Paralaxis 78clb (tree), Sean Pavone 16cra, Caio Pederneiras 79cra, Martin Pelanek 4tr, 61tl, Vadim Petrakov 98br, Pfeiffer 115c, photo-world 22cra, Alessia Pierdomenico 122tr, Kent Raney 54br, Scott E Read 61br, Roman023_photography 21br, S.Jeshurun Vineeth Roshan 144clb, Dmitrii Sakharov 121cb, Daniel Samray 77cla, sduraku 84ca, Vaclav Sebek 61crb, Sharky Photography 122ca, Sina Ettmer Photography 115clb, Dr Ajay Kumar Singh 2bl, 105br, Smarta 145tl, Solent News / Marko Korosec 41tl, Jiri-Sykora 53br, Jevon telesford 49tc, Travelsewhere 119crb, trgrowth 26-27b, TRphotos 118tc, Christian Vinces 70cb, 174tl, Westend61 on Offset 165crb, Wirestock Creators 2tl, 101ca, Faiz Zaki 61c; **Unsplash:** Brian Kairuz 150cla, William Olivieri 150tr, Sergey Pesterev 143cra